PLAYS BY NAOMI WALLACE

Please read
"War Boys" – p. 115.
I hope to be able to
produce it as part
of a Series on
"Borders" —
        with best wishes,
                Sallie

BROADWAY PLAY PUBLISHING INC
56 E 81st St., NY NY 10028-0202
212 772-8334 fax: 212 772-8358
http://www.BroadwayPlayPubl.com

First printing: December 1997
ISBN: 0-88145-135-5

Book design: Marie Donovan
Word processing: Microsoft Word for Windows
Typographic controls: Xerox Ventura Publisher 2.0 PE
Typeface: Palatino
Copy editing: Liam Brosnahan
Printed on recycled acid-free paper and bound in the USA

CONTENTS

ABOUT THE AUTHOR

Naomi Wallace is from Kentucky. Her plays include BIRDY, an adaptation for the stage of William Wharton's novel, which opened on the West End in London at the Comedy Theater in March 1997 and in Athens, Greece, at the same time; SLAUGHTER CITY, which was awarded the 1995 Mobil Prize, received its world premiere in January 1996 at the Royal Shakespeare Company and was subsequently presented by the American Repertory Theater in Cambridge, Massachusetts; IN THE HEART OF AMERICA, which received its world premiere at the Bush, was subsequently produced at the Long Wharf Theater under the direction of Tony Kushner and in Dortmund, Germany, was published in *American Theater* magazine, and was awarded the 1995 Susan Smith Blackburn Prize; IN THE SWEAT, cowritten with Bruce McLeod; IN THE FIELDS OF ACELDAMA; THE GIRL WHO FELL THROUGH A HOLE IN HER SWEATER, a children's play cowritten with Bruce McLeod, which was produced by the London New Play Festival; and WAR BOYS, which was produced at London's Finborough Theater.

Her film, LAWN DOGS, has been directed by John Duigan (FLIRTING, SIRENS), is produced by Duncan Kenworthy (FOUR WEDDINGS AND A FUNERAL), and will be distributed by Rank Films in 1997.

A published poet in both England and the United States, she received the National Poetry Competition award, the Nation's Discovery Award, as well as grants from the Kentucky Foundation for Women and the Kentucky Arts Council. Her monologue, THE FISH STORY, was published in MONOLOGUES BY WOMEN FOR WOMEN: 1994. Her book of poetry, TO DANCE A STONY FIELD, was published in the United Kingdom in May 1995. BIRDY has been published by Faber and Faber. ONE FLEA SPARE has been published by Broadway Play Publishing Inc.

At present, Wallace is under commission by the Royal Shakespeare Company, Actors Theater of Louisville, and the Royal National Theater/B T Youth Project.

IN THE HEART OF AMERICA

ORIGINAL PRODUCTION

IN THE HEART OF AMERICA had its first performance on 3 August 1994 at the Bush Theater in London. The cast and creative contributors were:

Richard Dormer
Robert Glenister
Sasha Hails
Toshie Ogura
Zubin Varla

Director .... Dominic Dromgoole
Design .... Angela Davis
Lighting ....Paul Russell

CHARACTERS & SETTING

CRAVER PERRY
FAIROUZ SABOURA
LUE MING
REMZI SABOURA
BOXLER

TIME

The present and the past

PLACE

A motel room, a military camp in Saudi Arabia, another room, the Iraqi desert

SET

Minimal and not "realistic"

And I await those who return,
who come knowing my times of death.
I love you when I love you not.
The walls of Babylon are close
in the daylight, and your eyes
are big, and your face looms
large in the light.

It is as if you have not been born yet,
we have not separated, and you
have not felled me, as if above
the storm tops every speech is
beautiful, every reunion,
a farewell.

Mahmoud Darwish

ACT ONE

Scene One

(Lights up on CRAVER *doing a headstand.* FAIROUZ *is standing in the shadows, watching.)*

FAIROUZ: He sent me a horn in a box. It was a ram's horn.

CRAVER: He is a funny guy.

FAIROUZ: Do you laugh at him?

CRAVER: *(Gets to his feet)* What did you say your name was?

FAIROUZ: I don't laugh at him.

CRAVER: What's your background? He's never clear where he's from.

FAIROUZ: Can you tell me how he's doing?

CRAVER: I told you over the phone I haven't heard from him in months.

FAIROUZ: You are his best friend.

CRAVER: I'm sorry to hear that.

FAIROUZ: Where is he? *(Beat)* Mr Craver.

CRAVER: Perry. Mr Perry. Craver's my first name. C-R-A-V-E-R. How did you get my address?

FAIROUZ: Remzi wrote in a letter...

CRAVER: I hardly know him.

FAIROUZ: He wrote: "Craver and I are never separate."

CRAVER: People get lost. Call the Army.

FAIROUZ: I did.

CRAVER: *(Does another headstand)* This kid over in Saudi taught me how to do this. It's not keeping your legs in the air; it's how you breathe. See? You got to push the air up through your lungs and into your feet. Then your feet will stay up, float like balloons.

FAIROUZ: Can Remzi do that? Stand on his head like you?

CRAVER: *(Stands)* Remzi has no balance.

FAIROUZ: He wrote me that he loved you.

CRAVER: And who do you love?

FAIROUZ: I threw it out. The ram's horn.

CRAVER: We must have bought a dozen horns while we were over there, but not one of them was good enough to send her. He wrote her name on the inside of it. F-A-I-R-O-U-Z. Fairouz. That was the name he wrote.

FAIROUZ: It had a bad smell.

CRAVER: Fairouz isn't anything like you.

FAIROUZ: Horns make noise.

CRAVER: He said she was like a flower.

FAIROUZ: I don't like noise. Remzi knows that.

CRAVER: No, he said she was like milk, sweet, fresh milk.

FAIROUZ: He likes to race. Did he race with you? He's not fast but he won't believe it.

CRAVER: Fairouz would have appreciated his gift.

FAIROUZ: Do you expect me to beg you?

CRAVER: Know what we call Arabs over there?

FAIROUZ: I'm not afraid of you, Mr Perry. When I find out, I'll be back. *(She exits.)*

CRAVER: *(Calls after her)* Fairouz! *(Beat)* He was my friend.

Scene Two

(CRAVER asleep, worn out. A figure of a woman—an apparition or perhaps something more real—enters. CRAVER wakes.)

CRAVER: Are you looking for him too?

LUE MING: I might be. Who?

CRAVER: Remzi. Remzi Saboura.

LUE MING: Are you Mr Calley?

CRAVER: No. I'm not.

LUE MING: Oh my. I'm in the wrong house.

CRAVER: How did you get in?

LUE MING: I was homing in on a small jewelry store in Columbus, Georgia. Is this Georgia?

CRAVER: Kentucky. Motel 6.

LUE MING: And you're not Calley?

CRAVER: Are you Chinese?

LUE MING: Oh no. I was born in Hanoi.

CRAVER: What are you doing here?

LUE MING: I've never left my country. I'm a real homebody.

CRAVER: You speak good English.

LUE MING: Haven't tried it before, but it's going nicely, isn't it?

CRAVER: What do you want?

LUE MING: He's about five foot ten, red in the face, and likes colorful fish. He should be in his fifties by now.

CRAVER: I'm not Calley. I can't help you.

LUE MING: (Sniffs) A trace. Yes. You smell of him. He's your buddy. Who are you?

CRAVER: Craver Perry.

LUE MING: What do you do?

CRAVER: Not much right now. I'm...on leave.

LUE MING: Ah. An Army fellow. Where were you stationed in Vietnam?

CRAVER: Vietnam? I wasn't in Vietnam. I was in the Gulf. In Saudi. In Iraq?

LUE MING: How can they fight in Vietnam and the Gulf at the same time?

CRAVER: We're not fighting in Vietnam.

LUE MING: Of course you are. Why, just yesterday my grandfather was out in the fields trying to pull a calf out of the mud. The rains. So much rain. You flew over with your plane and bang, bang, bang, one dead cow and one dead grandfather.

CRAVER: I've never even been to Vietnam.

LUE MING: Of course you have.

CRAVER: The Vietnam war ended over fifteen years ago, lady.

LUE MING: Are you sure?

CRAVER: Positive.

LUE MING: Who won? My God, who won?

CRAVER: You did.

LUE MING: Oh I wish I could have told Grandpa that this morning. *(Beat)* So I missed the house and the year. But not the profession. How many gooks have you killed?

CRAVER: I don't kill gooks; I kill Arabs.

LUE MING: Really? Arabs?

CRAVER: Not just any Arabs, Iraqi Arabs. Saddam Arabs. But that war is over now too.

LUE MING: Who won?

CRAVER: We had a kill ratio of a thousand to one.

LUE MING: Oh my! *(Beat)* What's it like to kill a woman?

CRAVER: I never killed anyone.

LUE MING: Such modesty! In my village alone you killed sixteen people, seven pigs, three cows, and a chicken.

CRAVER: I never killed anyone in my life. I never got that close.

LUE MING: Does it feel the same to shoot a cow in the back as it does to shoot a man in the back?

CRAVER: Get the fuck out of my room.

LUE MING: Lue Ming. *(Caresses his face)* I can't leave now! I think we're falling in love.

Scene Three

(A year earlier in the Saudi desert. CRAVER *and* REMZI *in positions to sprint.)*

REMZI: I get more traction running on this sand.

CRAVER: Get on your marks.

REMZI: Like a streak of light I'll pass you by, Craver. Just watch.

CRAVER: Get set!

REMZI: You just watch me.

CRAVER: Go!

REMZI: Wait! Wait! Cramp. Shit.

CRAVER: Bad luck to get beat before we start.

REMZI: I'm going to visit the village where my parents were born. When I get my first leave. Want to come with me?

CRAVER: Nope.

REMZI: Don't like to be seen with Arabs. Look. I've got more money than you. You're broke and I'm Arab. That about evens it out, doesn't it?

CRAVER: The C B U-75 carries eighteen hundred bomblets, called Sad Eyes. Sad Eyes.

REMZI: What do you think it's like...

CRAVER: One type of Sad Eyes can explode before hitting the ground.

REMZI: ...to kill someone?

CRAVER: Each bomblet contains six hundred razor-sharp steel fragments.

REMZI: I wonder what I'll feel like after I do it?

CRAVER: It's nothing personal: We're not just here to get them out of Kuwait, but to protect a way of life.

REMZI & CRAVER: Flawed it may be, but damn well worth protecting!

CRAVER: Those poor bastards are so brainwashed by Saddam, they need to kill like we need oxygen.

REMZI: When I went in for the interview, the recruiter asked me was I against taking another person's life.

CRAVER: If you are, you could fuck up an entire war.

REMZI: I just went in for the interview to piss my mother and sister off. The recruiter said: "What you need, son, is all right here." He looked at me, and I looked back. Then he said something that changed my life: "The Army will give you a quiet sense of pride."

CRAVER: "A quiet sense of pride." *(Beat)* I'm not going to die.

REMZI: I am.

CRAVER: It's hot here. Why does it have to be so hot here? Can't we just turn the sun up a few degrees and roast those motherfuckers! All these weeks with our ass frying in the sun, crawling through the sand like mutts, and the drills, drills, drills. Tomorrow might be the real thing. *(Beat)* We've got eight types of guided bombs.

REMZI: I wonder if you'll see it.

CRAVER: There's the G M-130, an electro-optically or infrared two-thousand-pound powered bomb. See what?

REMZI: How I die.

CRAVER: Then there's the G B U-10 Paveway II, a two-thousand-pound laser-guided bomb based on an M K-84.

REMZI: Let's say I'm lying over there, dead as can be, and then you see it's me, from a distance. But you still have to walk over to my body to check it out. So, how would you walk?

CRAVER: We've got Harm missiles, Walleyes, Clusters, and guided anti-tanks.

REMZI: Craver. This is something important I'm talking about. Let's say I'm you and I see me lying up ahead, dead. I stop in my tracks. I'm upset. We were friends, and I've got to cross the thirty or so feet between us. *(Does a 'walk' over to the imaginary dead body)* No. That feels too confident.

CRAVER: And you wouldn't feel confident because...

REMZI: Because I'd be thinking: That could just as easily be me lying there as him.

CRAVER: Right. So maybe you'd do it like this. Kind of... *(Does his 'walk' up to the imaginary body)*

REMZI: That's too careful.

CRAVER: Yeah. And too scared. I mean, I might be feeling in a pretty nice way, thinking about being alive and not quite as dead as you.

REMZI: You've got a point there. You might be feeling pretty O K.

CRAVER: And fucking lucky too, 'cause the blood's still rolling through my veins.

REMZI: Something like this maybe. *(Does another 'walk', a sort of combination of his others)*

CRAVER: Yes! That's it! That's it! Let me try. O K. I see you up ahead of me, twenty feet, maybe thirty, and I want to get closer to you....Why do I want to get closer if you're dead and I know it's you? I mean, there's nothing else to figure out then, is there?

REMZI: Because....I'm your friend, and you'd rather be the one to report my death than some jerk who doesn't know I exist.

CRAVER: Right. So here I go.

REMZI: Get on your mark.

CRAVER: Get set.

REMZI: Go!

CRAVER: *(Copies REMZI's walk, but not quite as well)* That didn't feel right.

REMZI: Your shoulders are too tight. Loosen up. See it before you, my body up ahead.

CRAVER: How did you die?

REMZI: This Iraqi we shot dead isn't dead. He's almost dead, but he's got just enough strength to fire one more time. When I turn my back—bang! —he shoots me.

CRAVER: Where?

REMZI: In the neck.

CRAVER: Got it.

REMZI: So there I am in the sand, a bullet in my neck.

CRAVER: And it's hot. A fucking hot day, and the sun is pissing a hole through my fucking hot head.

REMZI: Exactly, and I'm dead.

CRAVER: But I'm alive.

REMZI: And glad to be that way.

CRAVER: But you were my buddy. We were friends...just friends or good friends?

REMZI: Pretty good friends.

CRAVER: Pretty good friends.

REMZI: Right. And now you have to cross the distance between us.

CRAVER: About thirty-five feet.

REMZI: And then you do it. The walk. The shortest and most important walk of your life. And you have to believe you can do it, with dignity in your stride, power, and above all, a quiet sense of pride.

CRAVER: I'm ready.

REMZI: So am I.

(They link arms and walk in unison.)

Scene Four

(FAIROUZ is also practicing a walk.)

FAIROUZ: Keep your chin in the air at all times. As though your chin has a string attached to it that is pulling it up.

(LUE MING appears and walks in unison behind her. FAIROUZ doesn't yet notice her.)

FAIROUZ: No, a hook is better, a hook in your chin like a fish. Beauty lesson number seven: walking with grace.

LUE MING: It's all a matter of balance.

FAIROUZ: Not you again. I told you I don't know Calley.

LUE MING: Your friend Craver said you might know.

FAIROUZ: He's not my friend.

LUE MING: Are we still in Kentucky?

FAIROUZ: Yes.

LUE MING: American boys are so interesting! Full of secrets. All roads lead through him. My road. Your road. Dominoes in the dark.

FAIROUZ: Have you tried the other motel, across the street?

LUE MING: Calley's a soldier. A lieutenant. Of Charlie Company. A unit of the American Division's 11th Light Infantry Brigade. Very light. So light some thought he was an angel when he came home.

FAIROUZ: How do the women walk in your country?

LUE MING: Not as upright as we'd like. Hunched over a bit most of the time.

FAIROUZ: Show me.

LUE MING: *(She shows her)* The lower a body is to the ground, the less of a target.

FAIROUZ: I can't move without making noise. Clump, clump, clump. My mother always wanted me to walk with what she calls "presence". When I was in the fourth grade I had to walk home from school.

LUE MING: Show me. How you walked home from school.

FAIROUZ: It was only three blocks. *(She walks again.)*

LUE MING: Yes. I think I remember it now.

(Now they are both practicing their walks.)

FAIROUZ: There were some older children in the seventh grade. Two boys and a girl. They stopped me on the sidewalk. They wanted me to take off my shoes.

LUE MING: You should meet my mother; she has one foot.

FAIROUZ: To see the toes.

LUE MING: She stepped on a mine on her way for a piss.

FAIROUZ: Not the toes, but the hooves. They said I had hooves for toes. Devil's feet.

LUE MING: It was March 16, 1968.

FAIROUZ: Devil's feet.

LUE MING: Why, you weren't even born then, were you?

FAIROUZ: *(Chants)* Devil's feet. Devil's feet.

LUE MING: Devil's feet?

FAIROUZ: Yes. *(Chants)* Fairouz has devil's feet.

LUE MING: *(Chants)* Dirty Arab devil, you go home.

FAIROUZ: *(Chants)* Dirty Arab devil, you go home!

LUE MING: Get her shoe. Pull off her shoe.

FAIROUZ: Hold her down and pull off her shoe!

FAIROUZ & LUE MING: *(Chant)* Dirty Arab, dirty Arab, you go home!

FAIROUZ: Remzi! *(Beat)* Remzi.

LUE MING: Arab! Slope! Dink!

FAIROUZ: No. They didn't call me that: slope.

LUE MING: Thought I'd throw it in. Slope. Dink. Gook.

FAIROUZ: "Gook" I've heard of.

LUE MING: The Philippines war. It was used again for Korea, and then recycled for Vietnam. How did they get your shoe off?

FAIROUZ: I can't remember. I can figure the distance from right here, where we're standing, to the center of the earth, but I can't remember just how the shoe came off.

LUE MING: But it did come off? And when they saw you didn't have devil's feet did they let you be their friend?

FAIROUZ: A happy ending? It was for them. I think they were scared of me. Afterwards, they weren't.

LUE MING: And now you have a devil's foot?

FAIROUZ: It does look a bit like a hoof now. The bones curved wrong. Do you know what's happened to my brother?

LUE MING: I think we met each other once, but we were headed in different directions.

FAIROUZ: My God, where? Where did you see him?

LUE MING: I don't know anymore. We passed each other in a rather bad storm, and he reached out and touched my sleeve. Then he was gone.

FAIROUZ: Thank God. He's alive.

LUE MING: I didn't say that, my dear.

FAIROUZ: *(Not listening)*: He's alive!

Scene Five

(A year earlier. REMZI and FAIROUZ are talking. FAIROUZ is polishing his combat boots.)

FAIROUZ: You're becoming a stranger.

REMZI: Look. I'm sorry about the occupation and that you don't feel you have a homeland, but I do. And it's here. Not over there in some never-never land.

FAIROUZ: I hardly recognize you.

REMZI: Iraq invaded a sovereign country. That's against international law.

FAIROUZ: International law? Ha! Your own land is overrun, occupied, slowly eaten up....

REMZI: *(Mocks)* Village by village, orchard by orchard. Decades and decades of U N resolutions...

FAIROUZ: And no one's ever smacked a Desert Shield on those bastards!

REMZI: There's just no parallel.

FAIROUZ: There's always a parallel. Did mother ever tell you how she broke her hip before she came to America?

REMZI: She fell down when she was running away from the soldiers...

FAIROUZ: No. She was running toward the soldiers.

REMZI: I've heard this so many times it's a sweet little lullaby that could rock me to sleep. So mother saved father and they broke her hip with a rifle butt. Crack, crack. Bone broke. Hobble, hobble for the rest of her life. What do you expect me to do, hobble around for the rest of my life? You're so serious. Open your mouth and laugh for a change. You used to do that, remember? Get out of the house. Throw a party. Go to the Burger King on the corner and order some fries. *(Beat)* You're an American girl. Enjoy it.

FAIROUZ: I'm an Arab woman.

REMZI: You've never even been there.

FAIROUZ: Neither have you!

REMZI: If you walked into our village today, they'd tar and feather you.

FAIROUZ: Fuck you. I'd put on a veil.

REMZI: The veil's not the problem. You haven't been a virgin since you were thirteen.

FAIROUZ: How dare you!

REMZI: I'm sorry.

FAIROUZ: I was at least fourteen! *(They laugh.)*

FAIROUZ: Mother still says to me "The honor of a girl is like a piece of glass. If it's broken, you can never glue it together again."

REMZI: Why don't you tell her the truth?

FAIROUZ: It's my truth. Not hers. You hardly know her, and she lives five minutes away!

REMZI: I can't talk to her.

FAIROUZ: Learn Arabic.

REMZI: No. She should learn English. She's been here over twenty years.

FAIROUZ: She speaks English. She just won't.

REMZI: You're still doing the shopping for her, aren't you?

(FAIROUZ *doesn't answer.*)

REMZI: You should move out.

FAIROUZ: In the stores, for years, she'd lift me in her arms, and whisper in my ear "chubbes."

REMZI: "Chubbes."

FAIROUZ: And I would say "bread." "Halib", and I would say "milk."

REMZI: "Halib."

FAIROUZ: She's our mother.

REMZI: You were going to be a nurse, a doctor, or something. Get your degree. Get a job. I want a quiet life. As an American citizen. That's good enough for me. Beats living in the past.

FAIROUZ: An American citizen. What is that? This government pays for the guns that force us off our land.

REMZI: *(Interrupts)* Allah, spare me! Jesus Christ! It's not my land. I'm not into redrawing maps or being trapped in the minds of crusty grandparents.

FAIROUZ: We're your family.

REMZI: Some family. More like a selection of Mesopotamian ruins.

FAIROUZ: Why don't you learn a little something about—

REMZI: About ruins?

FAIROUZ: The Intifada?

REMZI: What? They're finally letting the women out of their houses to throw stones?

FAIROUZ: We throw stones. We run unions. We go to prison. We get shot.

REMZI: Oh, martyrdom! Why don't you get out of the house and throw a few stones around here! You've got a big mouth, Fairouz, but your world is this small. I'm sick of being a hyphen: the Palestinian, the gap between Arab-American. There's room for me here. Where I have my friends.

FAIROUZ: Ah, yes. Your friends. You tell your friends I was born that way.

REMZI: You're going to blame me that no one wants to marry a girl with a gimpy foot.

FAIROUZ: My foot is deformed, but my cunt works just fine!

REMZI: You have a mouth full of dirt, sister. What is it you want from me?

FAIROUZ: What I want? *(She speaks some angry lines to him in Arabic.)*

REMZI: Gibberish, Fairouz. Save it for the relatives.

(FAIROUZ *speaks another line of Arabic to him.*)

REMZI: I'm not a refugee. It's always somewhere else with you, always once removed. I am not scattered.

FAIROUZ: If I could go to war with you, I'd shoot my enemies first, then I'd shoot the ones who made them my enemies.

REMZI: Enemies. Always the enemies.

FAIROUZ: There are three kinds of people. Those who kill. Those who die. And those who watch. Which one are you, Remzi? Which one are you? I know. I know which one you are, don't I?

REMZI: Go to hell. I was a kid. A child. You'll never let it go, will you?

FAIROUZ: I just don't want you to join up without knowing that sometimes I still hate you.

Scene Six

(A year earlier in the Saudi desert. REMZI *and* CRAVER *are doing jumping jacks.* BOXLER *enters.)*

BOXLER: That's enough. Take a rest.

REMZI & CRAVER: Yes, Lieutenant.

BOXLER: At ease.

CRAVER: Thank you, sir.

BOXLER: No sirs and thank-yous. We're equal when I say at ease. Where are you girls from? Haven't seen you around.

CRAVER: Echo Company A, 2, 3, sir.

REMZI: Those fatigues you have on. I don't think I've seen those kind before.

BOXLER: Special Forces.

CRAVER: I can smell the mothballs.

BOXLER: I like a sense of humor. *(To* REMZI*)* Where are you from, babe?

REMZI: The States.

BOXLER: I mean, where are your parents from?

REMZI: My father died when I was just a kid. My mother never told me where she was from.

BOXLER: Now that's not nice....Parents owe the knowledge of their roots to their sons. A root must know its origins. You, my son, are a root living in the dark without a compass, and you have no idea what kind of tree is going to sprout forth from your skull. I'd say, American Indian, maybe. No. Could be your Mommy is from Pakistan. Then again, could be South of the Border. It's hard to tell these days.

REMZI: Yes. It is.

BOXLER: But never mind. We're all family here, aren't we?

CRAVER: Do you know about the Sad Eyes, sir?

BOXLER: Boxler's my name. And of course I know about the Sad Eyes. I've seen them on the faces of many a soldier who comes back without his buddy at his side.

CRAVER: The weapon. Sad Eyes is a weapon.

BOXLER: That's what I love about war. The creativity of it. *(Beat)* Shall we?

CRAVER & REMZI: Ready, sir.

BOXLER: *(As he speaks he takes out a blindfold and puts it on. He gets to his knees.)* Now, let's say you have a situation. A delicate situation. You've taken an Iraqi prisoner. He has a secret, and you need to get this secret without breaking international law, the Geneva Constrictions, etc. Prisoners must be treated humanely. Please tie my hands behind my back.

(No response)

BOXLER: Do as I tell you. Use your handkerchief.

(REMZI does so.)

BOXLER: All right. Interrogate me.

(Neither CRAVER nor REMZI responds.)

BOXLER: Bang, crash! Rat-tat-tat-tat! Howl! There are bullets flying all around you. This camel jockey knows where the reserve forces are located, and, if they aren't destroyed, you and your buddies are minced meat. *(Beat)* Interrogate me!

REMZI: What's your name? I said: What's your name? He won't talk, Craver. What do we do?

BOXLER: Be firm.

CRAVER: Tell us your name, shit bag, and we'll go easy on you.

(No response from BOXLER.)

CRAVER: Give him a push.

BOXLER: That's an idea. Go on.

(REMZI *pushes him, but not hard.*)

BOXLER: That's a start.

(CRAVER *does so, but harder.*)

BOXLER: You two Barbies, you think just because you push me around a little I'm going to spill my guts? You're nothing but piss-ants with one hand tied behind your back.

(CRAVER *shoves him, and he falls over.*)

REMZI: One hand tied behind our backs?

(He strikes BOXLER. CRAVER *strikes him too.)*

BOXLER: You two dandelions aren't getting anywhere. Hey, baby doll, yeah you, the one with the dark skin, are you a half-breed?

REMZI: No. But you are. *(He kicks* BOXLER *in the stomach.)* You fucking sandnigger.

BOXLER: From what I can see of your face, you're a sandnigger yourself.

(REMZI *kicks* BOXLER *again.*)

BOXLER: What a farce: a sandnigger killing sandniggers.

(REMZI *keeps kicking until* BOXLER *lies still.*)

(Some moments of silence)

REMZI: Sir? Did I hurt you, sir?

(BOXLER *doesn't move.*)

CRAVER: Oh shit.

(REMZI *and* CRAVER *free* BOXLER's *wrists and eyes.* BOXLER *springs to his feet, unharmed.*)

BOXLER: *(To* REMZI*)* That was good. For a first time.

(Suddenly he punches REMZI *in the stomach.)*

BOXLER: Pity is what you leave behind you, son, back home, tucked under your pillow with your teddy bear and girly magazine. Now get to your feet, you stinking Arab.

(REMZI *starts to get up, but* BOXLER *pushes him over with his foot.* REMZI *attacks* BOXLER, *but* BOXLER *restrains him.*)

BOXLER: That's it. That's it. Now hold on to it! Hold on to that anger. Stoke it. Cuddle it, and, when the right moment comes, take aim and let it fly. A soldier without anger is a dead soldier.

CRAVER: What about me, sir?

BOXLER: What about you?

CRAVER: How do I get that anger when I need it?

BOXLER: Where are you from?

CRAVER: Town of Hazard. Kentucky. Sir.

BOXLER: Let me see your teeth? Hmmm. Trash, are you?

CRAVER: Yes, sir.

BOXLER: Joined up because you couldn't get a job.

CRAVER: Yes, sir.

BOXLER: Father dead?

CRAVER: Yes, sir. The mines, sir.

BOXLER: Burned to a crisp in an explosion?

CRAVER: Suffocated. His lungs, sir.

BOXLER: A pity you weren't with him when he died.

CRAVER: It was like something sawing through wood. His breathing, sir. I couldn't stand to hear it. But the Company wouldn't let him retire. He kept working. For the money, sir. We had to tie him into his chair to keep him at home.

BOXLER: Shat right there in his chair, did he? And you let your mother clean up his mess. Never offered her a hand. Tsk, tsk. Went out with your friends and got drunk on Pabst Blue Ribbon. But one night you came home early, and he was still sitting there, tied to his chair. Your mother was passed out on the couch.

REMZI: Sir, this is ridicu—

BOXLER: *(Interrupts)* Yes, it is, isn't it? Because Craver then leaned over and said into his father's ear: "I'm sorry, Dad. I am so sorry." And do you know, Remzi, just what his father did to show his acceptance and respect for his prodigal son? He pissed. Right then and there. Pissed where he sat, and Craver didn't even know it until he looked down and saw he was standing in it. The piss soaked through his shoes, right into his socks.

CRAVER: When he went into the mines he was my father. When he came back out, he was something else. I couldn't love something else.

BOXLER: And you were out fucking some pretty little box in the back of his Ford pickup truck the night he drew his last, painful breath. You shot your cum the moment his heart stopped.

REMZI: *(To CRAVER)*: Don't listen to him, Craver.

CRAVER: That's where you're wrong. I didn't come. I never came.

BOXLER: And why not? *(Beat)* What was the problem? Are you a funny little boy, one of those ha-ha little boys?

CRAVER: What are you going to do about it? Report me? I'll break your fucking neck.

REMZI: Let's get out of here, Crave. *(CRAVER shoves REMZI away.)*

REMZI: *(To CRAVER)* My, my. I can call your father a broken-down, coal-shitting, piss-poor excuse for the American dream and you don't bat an eye, but when I detect that you're a bit on the queer side...

BOXLER: Craver?

(CRAVER suddenly turns on REMZI. They push each other. CRAVER knocks REMZI down and begins to choke REMZI.)

REMZI: Craver! Fuck! Craver!

BOXLER: *(Whispers)* Faggot. Shit-fucker.

REMZI: Stop it! Get off of me.

BOXLER: Sodomite. Fairy. *(Beat)* Feel it? Feel it inside you, Mr Perry? Now grab hold of it.

(BOXLER pulls CRAVER off of REMZI.)

BOXLER: Catch it. Hold it like a bullet between your teeth. And when the right moment comes, when you've spotted your enemy, let it rip, my son. Let it rip. But remember, aim is everything and unbridled anger is of no use to you, it's like crude oil: worthless without refinement. But you've got to know where to direct it. Out there, my friend. Out there, in Indian territory, beyond the sand dunes where the camels lie in wait. Think of them as culprits in the death of your father. If the ragheads hadn't shot our buffalo, we could have swapped them for their camels, and then we wouldn't have needed the coal mines to begin with, and your father would have worked in an auto factory, and he'd still be alive today.

CRAVER: That's not how it happened. *(Beat)* Sir.

BOXLER: You can give his death any reason you want. Facts are not infallible. They are there to be interpreted in a way that's useful to you. Why, your President does it, and he is no smarter than you. President Johnson says:

REMZI: President Bush.

BOXLER: Whatever the hell his name is, he said: "Our troops...will not be asked to fight with one hand tied behind their back". As you did in Vietnam. *(Begins to laugh)* Do you know how many tons of bombs were dropping on Vietnam? Four million six hundred thousand. It's awesome, isn't it?

REMZI: This is a different war, sir.

BOXLER: The tonnage dropped by the Allies in World War II was only three million. Now, my hands won't be tied behind my back when we go into Panama City. Operation Just Because, it will be called.

CRAVER: It was called Operation Just Cause. Just Cause.

REMZI: That was in '89. In December.

BOXLER: I'll be driving a tank there. They promised me I could drive a tank this time. The only nuisance is that crunching sound under my treads. A crunching sound, like this. *(Makes the sound)* Civilians have so little consideration.

CRAVER: You were never in Panama, sir.

REMZI: There were no civilian deaths to speak of.

BOXLER: But not to speak of, I'd say about three thousand. Now, when we went into the barrios of Grenada...

REMZI: Just where haven't you been, sir?

CRAVER: To hell. He hasn't been to hell, but he's on his way there.

BOXLER: Oh, there you're wrong. I stood outside the gates for a very long time. In rain and snow, fire and brimstone, but they wouldn't let me in. I don't know why they won't let me in.

(We hear LUE MING's voice offstage calling)

LUE MING: Fairouz! Fairouz!

BOXLER: Now we're ready for lesson two. How to handle women in combat.

(LUE MING calls "Where are you?" in Vietnamese.)

BOXLER: Hear it?

(REMZI and CRAVER do not hear it. BOXLER begins to slink away.)

BOXLER: Can't you hear it? Poor hound. She's still after me. Still sniffing at my tracks.

FAIROUZ: *(Offstage, calling)* Remzi! Remzi!

Scene Seven

(FAIROUZ is blindfolded. She moves about the dark stage carrying small paper lanterns. Throughout the scene LUE MING moves about the stage, taking up different positions in relation to FAIROUZ—here, now there—sometimes surprising FAIROUZ with her voice. Just prior to FAIROUZ speaking, LUE MING begins to sing a Vietnamese lullaby.)

FAIROUZ: I can see through it anyway.

LUE MING: This is how we must operate: able to pinpoint the enemy even though we are almost blind. Night vision. Strategy where there should be none.

FAIROUZ: Like a bat?

LUE MING: If you like. Now. Think past the obstacles, that which hides your objective. Map out the lie of the land as you remember it and have never seen it.

FAIROUZ: And forget the motel carpet?

LUE MING: Hands up! Don't you know there's a war on? Keep your head. Look for what is not there.

FAIROUZ: Imagine the land I can't see.

LUE MING: Once, an American soldier called himself my brother.

FAIROUZ: Sounds like a friendly war.

LUE MING: In the first years the soldiers gave us toffee and boiled sweets.

FAIROUZ: By the rice paddies? In Saigon?

LUE MING: Tu Cung, actually. By the coast. *(Beat)* Rush always gave me gum, Juicy Fruit gum. He called me his little sis. Once he gave me a ribbon to put in my hair. I had very long hair, beautiful, thick hair that I wore in a braid down my back. *(Beat)* But one day Rush didn't bring any gum and he took out his knife and cut off my braid.

FAIROUZ: Was it a slow knife? Serrated are slow.

LUE MING: Oh no, it was a quick knife, a Rush knife, and he strapped my hair to the back of his helmet. His friends laughed and laughed. Rush looked so very silly with his camouflage helmet on and this long, black braid hanging down his back.

FAIROUZ: It was only hair.

LUE MING: I'd be careful if I were blindfolded.

FAIROUZ: I like it. I could go anywhere in the world right now, and to do it I wouldn't have to lift a finger.

(From the shadows, we hear the sound of REMZI's *footsteps.)*

LUE MING: Or a foot.

FAIROUZ: I'm four hundred and thirty miles from home. This is the first time I've been outside of Atlanta. The first time I've flown in a plane.

LUE MING: I despise flying. It puts my hair in a tangle.

FAIROUZ: Could you get a message to Remzi?

LUE MING: Your brother's not accepting messages these days.

FAIROUZ: I'm sorry, but I don't have time for your lost braid. What's done is done. My brother is alive, and we must think about the living and wait for my brother to send word. *(Beat)* I'm sick of waiting. And I can't stop waiting.

LUE MING: Those who wait, burn.

Scene Eight

(FAIROUZ and REMZI, a year earlier.)

FAIROUZ: Did you get the vaccines you needed?

REMZI: Yesterday.

FAIROUZ: Then everything's in order?

REMZI: All set to leave. The big adventure awaits me. Little brother goes to war.

FAIROUZ: When we were small, the children from our school would come to our house to have a look at my funny foot. You made them pay a dime each time they had a look.

REMZI: I split the profit with you, fifty-fifty.

FAIROUZ: It was my foot.

REMZI: It was my idea.

FAIROUZ: I used to lie awake at night, for years, dreaming of ways to kill you. I thought: If I kill him, there will be no one to hate. I was investing my hatred in you. It was a long-term investment. Really, I think you owe me some thanks.

REMZI: For hating me?

FAIROUZ: Yes. Then you wouldn't be surprised by the hate of the world.

CRAVER: *(Offstage)* Remzi! Remzi!

(CRAVER, offstage and "somewhere else", calls REMZI's name, and REMZI exits. LUE MING enters.)

FAIROUZ: Listen to me. You don't have the right balance. I do. You see, I love you, but I hate you too. I have to. Tightly, tightly. As though at any moment either of us could slip off this earth. Are you listening to me?

LUE MING: *(Answering as REMZI)* Yes, I am, Fairouz. I'm listening.

FAIROUZ: Go say goodbye to Mother. She's in her room, and she won't come out. She says they'll kill you. Just like they killed Father.

LUE MING: That was an accident, and you know it. He fell onto the lily pads and into the pond and drowned.

FAIROUZ: His face was messed up. As though he'd been hit many times.

LUE MING: Water can do that to a face.

FAIROUZ: I've told Mother that, Remzi. Over and over I've told her that it's the Iraqis you're going off to fight, but she keeps saying *(Speaks in Arabic and then translates)* "They'll kill him. The Yankees will kill him." Silly old woman. She's all mixed up.

Scene Nine

(A military camp in Saudi Arabia. REMZI is sitting alone and reciting.)

REMZI: Tabun. Mawid. Zbib, trab ahmar, dibs.

(CRAVER enters. He listens to REMZI awhile.)

REMZI: Maya, zir, foron.

CRAVER: Sounds like you had a good leave.

REMZI: Zbib, trab ahmar, dibs. Raisins. Red soil. Molasses.

CRAVER: Really? How amazing...

REMZI: I went to visit my father's village. On the western side of the Hebron Mountains. Al-Dawayima. According to my mother, there were five hundred and fifty-nine houses there.

CRAVER: I didn't know you were back.

REMZI: Tall grasses, wildflowers, scrubs. That's all that's there now. Dozers have flattened the houses.

CRAVER: When did you get back?

REMZI: I went to the refugee camp nearby, but I couldn't speak the language. I could point, though.

CRAVER: We went on alert a couple of times. Lucky we didn't start without you.

REMZI: A Palestinian farmer explained to me that there are three varieties of fig suitable for preserving—asmar, ashqar, abiyad. The black fig, the blonde, and the white. Craver. I was a tourist there. An outsider.

CRAVER: You're a Palestinian.

REMZI: One old woman took me in for coffee, because I didn't know anyone and had nowhere to go. She called me "Yankee Palestina." These people lose their homes. They live in poverty, and they're the enemies of the world. *(Throws CRAVER a bag of figs)* I brought that for you.

CRAVER: Nice you remembered I existed. I think of the three, I'm the white fig variety. How do you say it?

REMZI: Abiyad.

CRAVER: Yeah. Abiyad. *(He tastes a fig)* These are nasty.

REMZI: You're not eating them right. You don't just plug them in your mouth like a wad of chewing tobacco. You've got to eat them with a sense of purpose. *(He eats one)* With a sense of grace.

(CRAVER picks out another one.)

CRAVER: With a quiet sense of pride?

REMZI: Exactly.

(CRAVER eats it.)

CRAVER: Nastier than the first one.

REMZI: No. Look. You're gobbling.

CRAVER: Why didn't you buy me a souvenir, like a nice little prayer rug?

REMZI: Eating is like walking. My sister taught me that. There's a balance involved. You have to eat the fig gently. As though it were made of the finest paper. *(Puts a fig in his own hand)* Look. I'll put the fig in my hand, and, without touching my hand, you pick it up. Gently.

(CRAVER starts to use his fingers, but REMZI stops his hand.)

REMZI: With your mouth. *(Beat)* Go on. See if you can do it.

(CRAVER leans down to REMZI's open hand and very carefully and very slowly lifts the fig from REMZI's hand. CRAVER holds the fig between his lips.)

REMZI: Now take it into your mouth. Slowly.

(REMZI helps the fig inside CRAVER's mouth.)

REMZI: Slowly. There... Well. How does it taste now?

CRAVER: *(After some moments of silence)*: Did you take a lot of pictures?

REMZI: On the streets of Atlanta I've been called every name you can think of: pimp, terrorist, half-nigger, mongrel, spic, wop, even Jew-bastard. And to these people in this camp it didn't matter a damn that I was some kind of a mix. Some kind of a something else, born someplace in a somewhere else than my face said. Or something like that. Do you know what I mean?

CRAVER: Haven't any idea.

REMZI: So. What's on for tomorrow?

CRAVER: Drills. Red Alert. Stop. Go. Stop. Go.

REMZI: Every day it's any day now.

CRAVER: I just want it to start.

Scene Ten

(LUE MING *and* FAIROUZ *rehearsing for* FAIROUZ's *travels.* LUE MING *is wearing* REMZI's *boots.*)

LUE MING: Your shoulders are too tight. That's what they look for. Tight shoulders, pinched faces.

FAIROUZ: My face isn't pinched.

LUE MING: If you're going to find your brother, you have to cross borders. But not with sweat on your upper lip. Try it again. Not a care in the world. Right at home. (*She assumes the posture of an immigration officer.*) Passport? Hmmm. North American?

FAIROUZ: Yes, sir.

LUE MING: Tourist?

FAIROUZ: Yes.

LUE MING: How long? How long have you been a tourist?

FAIROUZ: Most of my life, sir.

LUE MING: (*Speaks as herself*) Don't be perverse. (*Speaks as officer*) First time out of the United States?

FAIROUZ: Yes.

LUE MING: Relatives here?

FAIROUZ: Yes. I mean, no. I mean I do, but they—

LUE MING: (*Interrupts*) Just what do you mean, Miss...Saboura?

FAIROUZ: My parents were born here.

LUE MING: Here? Born here?

FAIROUZ: Yes.

LUE MING: You mean right where I'm standing? (*She lifts her feet and looks under them.*)

FAIROUZ: (*Looks at* LUE MINGs *boots*): Yes. (*Beat*) Where did you get these?

LUE MING: Do you think they're stuck to my shoes?

FAIROUZ: I know these boots. What?

LUE MING: Your parents. Do you think they're stuck to my shoes?

FAIROUZ: I don't understand.

LUE MING: I assure you it was an accident. One minute they're alive, and, well, the next minute they're under my shoes.

FAIROUZ: My brother is lost.

LUE MING: Lucky man.

FAIROUZ: I'm Palestin—

LUE MING: Don't say it! Don't say it! It's like a bee that flies into my ear and fornicates there.

FAIROUZ: Don't you think you're overdoing it?

LUE MING: You must be prepared for them to throw anything at you. *(Beat)* Purpose of your visit?

FAIROUZ: Your ruins.

LUE MING: Yes. Lots of ruins. I like ruins. Your voice reminds me of one. Are you sad? Are you missing someone close to your heart? Pull up your shirt. I don't have all day.

(FAIROUZ raises her shirt.)

LUE MING: Education?

FAIROUZ: Doctor. I haven't finished the degree.

LUE MING: Ah, a person who quits?

FAIROUZ: I plan to go back.

LUE MING: You can't go back to Al-Dawayima. There's no place to go back to. *(Beat)* So you're Arab?

FAIROUZ: American.

LUE MING: American?

FAIROUZ: Arab.

LUE MING: Make up your mind!

FAIROUZ: I'm a Palestinian-Arab-American. From Atlanta. Sir.

Scene Eleven

(FAIROUZ enters CRAVER's motel room.)

FAIROUZ: Did he talk to you about his visit to the Territories?

CRAVER: Not a word.

FAIROUZ: He never likes to learn anything new.

CRAVER: Ever heard of the Beehive? It's the ultimate concept in improved fragmentation. It spins at high velocity, spitting out eighty-eight hundred fléchettes.

FAIROUZ: Fléchettes?

CRAVER: Tiny darts with razor-sharp edges capable of causing deep wounds.

FAIROUZ: What is a deep wound? How deep exactly?

CRAVER: To the bone. You should leave now.

FAIROUZ: I got a letter from the army.

CRAVER: Know the D U penetrator? Cigar-shaped, armor-piercing bullets. The core of the bullet is made from radioactive nuclear waste.

FAIROUZ: They say he's missing.

CRAVER: When fired, the D U's uranium core bursts into flame. Ever had forty tons of depleted uranium dumped in your backyard?

FAIROUZ: Not in action, just missing.

CRAVER: Things get lost. People—

FAIROUZ: Get lost. But why not you? Why didn't you get lost?

CRAVER: Because I fell in love. In our bunkers at night, Remzi used to read the names out loud to us, and it calmed us down. He must have read that weapons manual a hundred times. All those ways to kill the human body. Lullabies. It was like...they were always the same and always there, and when we said them to ourselves there was nothing else like it: Fishbeds, Floggers and Fulcrums. Stingers, Frogs, Silkworms, Vulcans, Beehives, and Bouncing Bettys.

FAIROUZ: Did you love my brother?

CRAVER: I can't remember.

FAIROUZ: But you can. You will. Remember!

CRAVER: I remember...what my first...favorite was: the B-52, the Buff. B-U-F-F. The Big Ugly Fat Fellow, it can carry up to sixty thousand pounds of bombs and cruise missiles.

FAIROUZ: All right. Let's try something more simple.

CRAVER: It has survived in front-line service for three generations.

FAIROUZ: Not about numbers, but about flesh.

CRAVER: It has an engine thrust of thirteen thousand seven hundred and fifty pounds and a maximum speed of five hundred and ninety-five miles per hour. It's slow but it's bad.

FAIROUZ: If you could give his flesh a velocity?

CRAVER: The Buffs, the B-52s, won the Gulf War. Not the smarts. Not the smarts.

FAIROUZ: Or a number, what would it be?

CRAVER: Ninety-three percent of the bombs dropped were free-falls from the bellies of Fat Fellows.

FAIROUZ: If you could give his flesh a number?

CRAVER: Only seven percent were guided, and, of these half-wits, forty percent missed their targets.

FAIROUZ: A number that's short of infinity? Was that your desire for him?

CRAVER: Forty...forty-five percent of the smarts...they missed...

FAIROUZ: Something short of infinity?

CRAVER: They missed their targets.

FAIROUZ: Did you or did you not fuck him?

CRAVER: That *(Beat)* is a lot of missed targets.

FAIROUZ: O K: Mr White Trash likes Arab ass, yes? Is it good? Is it sweet like white ass? Do you find it exotic?

CRAVER: I'm not that kind of a soldier.

FAIROUZ: He could be a bastard, my brother. But if you fucked him and then hurt him in any way, I'll tear your heart out.

CRAVER: Remzi never said he had a sister with a limp. His sister, he said she walked like a princess.

FAIROUZ: Was he gentle with you? Sometimes when we were children he would soak my foot in a bowl of warm water, with lemon and orange rinds. He would blow on my toes to dry them. He thought if he cared for my foot, day by day, and loved it, that somehow it would get better. *(Beat)* What was it like to kiss him?

CRAVER: After the Buffs it was the G R. M K-1 Jaguar with two Rolls-Royce Adour M K-102 turbofans. A fuselage pylon and four wing pylons can carry up to ten thousand pounds of armaments...

(REMZI now "appears." FAIROUZ moves away and watches, as though watching CRAVER's memory.)

CRAVER: The Jag can carry a mix of cannons, smarts, and gravity bombs. And get this: maximum speed: Mach 1.1.

CRAVER: Then there's the brain of the electronic warfare central nervous system: the E-3 Sentry, Boeing.

REMZI: If there ever was an indispensable weapon, it is the E-3 AWACS, capable of directing U N forces with tremendous accuracy. Improvements include:

CRAVER: A better Have Quick radar jamming system and an upgraded JTIDS. Able to manage hundreds of warplanes airborne at any given moment.

REMZI: At any given moment?

CRAVER: Any given moment.

REMZI: How about now?

CRAVER: We could go to jail. It's illegal in the Army.

REMZI: So are white phosphorous howitzer shells. So are fuel-air explosives.

CRAVER: We don't decide what gets dropped.

REMZI: Would you kiss me if I were dead?

CRAVER: Why would I kiss you if you were dead?

REMZI: Would you kiss me if I were alive?

CRAVER: I had a thing for the Sentry jet, but how long can love last, after the first kiss, after the second, still around after the third? I dumped the Sentry jet and went on to the Wild Weasel, F-4G. Like a loyal old firehorse, the Weasel was back in action.

REMZI: Have you ever touched the underbelly of a recon plane? Two General Electric J79-15 turbojets.

CRAVER: If you run your hand along its flank, just over the hip, to the rear end, it will go wet. Not damp but I mean wet.

REMZI: Have you ever run your face over the wing of an A-6 Intruder, or opened your mouth onto the tail of a A V-8B Harrier II? It's not steel you taste. It's not metal.

CRAVER: Ever had a Phoenix missile at the tip of your tongue? Nine hundred and eighty-five pounds of power, at launch.

(CRAVER *moves to kiss* REMZI, *but* REMZI *moves away.*)

FAIROUZ: Is that how you kissed him?

CRAVER: I kissed a girl for the first time when I was twelve. She had a mouth full of peanut butter and jelly and that's what I got. Have you ever seen an airplane take off vertically? That's what I was when I kissed Remzi, like the AV-8B Harrier II, straight up into the air, no runway, no horizontal run, but VTO, vertical takeoff.

FAIROUZ: Why don't you say it?

CRAVER: One Rolls-Royce turbojet going up, engine thrust twenty-one thousand five hundred pounds maximum speed.

FAIROUZ: Please. Just say it.

CRAVER: Forever. Remzi said to me the first time he kissed me: "What are you now, Craver Perry? A White Trash, River Boy, who kisses Arabs and likes it?" I said, "I'm a White Trash, River Boy, Arab-kissing Faggot." And the rest, as they say, is history. *(Beat)* Remzi was, as they say, history too.

FAIROUZ: Remzi is dead, isn't he?

CRAVER: I said he was history. That's something else.

FAIROUZ: How can this be funny to you?

CRAVER: If you saw your brother lying dead in the sand, just what would you say to him? Imagine it. There he is. Dead on the sand. A bullet in his neck.

FAIROUZ: Bled to death?

CRAVER: Maybe. What would you do?

(FAIROUZ touches his face.)

CRAVER: Like that? Would you touch Remzi like that? What if he didn't have a face? What if his face were gone too?

(She kisses CRAVER on the cheek.)

CRAVER: That would take a lot of guts if he didn't have a face.

FAIROUZ: What was it for? You're of no use to me. Just a dead brother now. Zero. No more Remzi to hate. No more Remzi...

CRAVER: ...to love. That's right. Do you think we're doing it too, falling in love?

FAIROUZ: *(Moves away from CRAVER)* Would Remzi like that? *(Beat)* Do you like to watch or do you like to kill? You haven't tried dying yet, have you? Perhaps you should.

CRAVER: There's nothing wrong with your foot.

FAIROUZ: You're kind. I see why Remzi was so attached to you.

(REMZI enters, unobserved by either of them.)

FAIROUZ: My brother was the kind that watched. Is he the other kind now, Mr Perry? *(Beat)* I think I'm going to scream.

(CRAVER backs away, watching the two of them, as though he is seeing them both in the past. REMZI holds her foot.)

REMZI: *(Talking to her gently)* Just once more.

FAIROUZ: I can't. I can't

REMZI: You've got to do it or you'll never walk right. Just once more.

FAIROUZ: Just once more. Only once more. Will it be better then?

REMZI: Soon. It will be better soon.

(REMZI *twists her foot, and she lets out a sound of pain that is part scream and part the low, deep sound of a horn.*)

END ACT ONE

ACT TWO

Scene One

(LUE MING *appears. She summons up the Gulf War: the sounds of jets, bombs, guns. The war sounds continue through the following invocation.*)

LUE MING: My sweet. My love. Come out from your hiding. Oh, my little angel, my tropical fish. Swim to me through the corridors of air. I am waiting for you. Come home. Come home.

(*The war sounds stop.*)

LUE MING: Yes. Yes. It's you.

(BOXLER *appears.*)

LUE MING: It is always, only you, could ever be you.

BOXLER: Boxler.

LUE MING: Is that it now, "Boxler"?

BOXLER: I have nothing to say to you.

LUE MING: You're looking so well. So robust. So alive. And happy?

BOXLER: When I'm training my girls.

LUE MING: And what do you teach them?

BOXLER: Are you enjoying your visit?

LUE MING: Some of your cities make me feel right at home. Burned out, bodies in the street, the troops restoring order. They're so much like Vietnam.

BOXLER: You're Vietcong, aren't you?

LUE MING: I hear your record sold over two hundred thousand copies. You're a pop star.

BOXLER: That was thirty...twenty-five...

LUE MING: Twenty-one years ago. Just how much time did you get?

BOXLER: I got labor for life, but three days later I was out of the stockade, courtesy of President Nick. Then I got thirty-five months in my bachelor pad at Fort Benning with my dog, my myna bird, and my tank full of tropical fish.

LUE MING: Could you sing it for me? That song?
(Sings the following to the tune of "The Battle Hymn of the Republic":)
My name is Rusty Calley
I'm a soldier of this land!

BOXLER: I'm a hero, you know. I'm a hero, and you're a dead gook.

LUE MING: Don't try to sweet-talk me. It won't work.

BOXLER: They took care of me. Friends in high places. I have a jewelry store and a Mercedes. I have a lot to be grateful for.

LUE MING: Have you missed me terribly?

BOXLER: I'm sorry, but I can't place you.

LUE MING: Take a look at my face, closely.

BOXLER: Nope.

LUE MING: You'll remember the walk. There is no one in the world who walks like Lue Ming. *(She walks.)*

BOXLER: Sorry.

LUE MING: How is it I can remember you and you can't remember me?

BOXLER: What's done is done.

LUE MING: And what's done is often done again and done again.

Scene Two

(REMZI and CRAVER are watching the bombs dropping over Baghdad from a long distance. We hear the muffled thuds of the bombs and see beautiful flashes of light far off.)

REMZI: One, two. And there. Three. Look at it. Cotton candy. Carnival. Dancing. Craver. You're missing it. That one! *(Beat)* "And all the king's horses and all the king's men..."

CRAVER: "Couldn't put Humpty together again."

(An even bigger flash of lights. CRAVER joins him. They both watch.)

REMZI: Do you think he really wanted to be whole again?

CRAVER: Who?

REMZI: The egg.

CRAVER: What?

REMZI: Do you think he wanted to be put back together?

CRAVER: How the hell should I know what an egg wants?

REMZI: I should be dead but I'm not.

(They see an awe-inspiring explosion.)

CRAVER: *(Sings)* Happy birthday, Baghdad.

REMZI: I think he was tired of being a good egg.

CRAVER: Make a wish.

REMZI: Yeah. A birthday.

CRAVER: If you sit out in the dark, they light up all around you. Like that. Back in Hazard. Just like that. All over the sky. Fireflies. There—

REMZI: That first time.

CRAVER: And then gone. There—

REMZI: Like. It was like—

CRAVER: And then gone.

REMZI: I was a window, and you put your hand through me.

Scene Three

*(*BOXLER *and* LUE MING*)*

BOXLER: You're not bad-looking.

LUE MING: I know.

BOXLER: But I could never touch you. I mean, really touch you. I mean I know you are human, but. Well. *(Beat)* I was a child once. Hard to believe, isn't it? I had blocks and crayons, and when it snowed I'd open my mouth to catch the flakes on my tongue. I had a favorite blanket. I liked most to roll the corner of it into a little point and stick it in my ear. Then I'd fall asleep. All the sounds around me were muffled and soft.

LUE MING: My three-year-old daughter had a blanket, made from two scarves my mother sewed together.

BOXLER: I had a father I loved and a mother I loved, and then I went to school.

LUE MING: Show me what you teach the boys. Show me.

BOXLER: My teacher made us sit in a formation, with the whitest faces up front in the first row, then the second and third rows for the olive skins and half-breeds, and the fourth and fifth rows for the dark ones.

LUE MING: Remember: You have a situation. *(She puts on a blindfold.)* You've captured a Vietcong, and you need to know the whereabouts of the others. Now be polite. You're an American soldier, and that means something.

BOXLER: Did you know they made bumper stickers with my name on it?

LUE MING: You know who I am.

BOXLER: Shut your squawking, bitch. *(Calls)* Hey, you two troopers. Over here on the double.

(REMZI and CRAVER enter.)

BOXLER: Remzi, what's the best way to make a woman talk?

CRAVER: The dozers are clearing the area, sir.

BOXLER: Get on with it. What dozers?

REMZI: We're mopping up.

BOXLER: I said make her talk!

CRAVER: Can you tell us where Saddam's minefields are?

BOXLER: This is Vietnam, son.

REMZI: We're in Iraq, sir.

BOXLER: This is Panama City!

CRAVER: We have the Dragon M-47 assault missile, sir. Couldn't we use that instead?

BOXLER: Duty is face-to-face confession, son. Between two people. You and this prisoner. Well, go on. Take down your pants.

CRAVER: Sir?

BOXLER: Take down your pants. *(To LUE MING)* Suck him.

LUE MING: *(To CRAVER)*: Haven't we met before?

BOXLER: Suck him, or I'll cut your head off.

(CRAVER unzips his pants. LUE MING begins to sing a Vietnamese lullaby.)

BOXLER: Jesus. Can't you even give her something to suck?

CRAVER: It's the singing, sir.

BOXLER: Remzi. Go get her kid. It's in the hut.

REMZI: What hut, sir? We're in the middle of a desert.

BOXLER: Get her fucking kid and bring it here, or I'll cut his dick off.

REMZI: What kid, sir?

BOXLER: What kid? There's always a kid.

LUE MING: The child is right here. In my arms. They all look at Lue Ming.

REMZI: We're moving out. Now, sir.

CRAVER: Remzi.

REMZI: Let's go.

(They exit. Silence.)

LUE MING: I so much prefer it like this. The two of us. Alone.

Scene Four

(A U S military camp somewhere in the Iraqi desert. REMZI and CRAVER are stunned and worn out.)

REMZI: Ancient Mesopotamia.

(CRAVER begins to whistle to the tune of "Armour Hot Dogs." Then REMZI joins him.)

CRAVER: *(Sings)* Hot dogs. Armour hot dogs. What kind of kids eat Armor hot dogs?

REMZI: *(Sings)* Fat kids, skinny kids, kids that climb on rocks.

CRAVER: *(Sings)* Tough kids, sissy kids, even kids with—

REMZI & CRAVER: *(Sing)* ...chicken pox! Love hot dogs. Armour hot dogs. The dogs kids love to bite.

CRAVER: I always loved that song when I was a kid.

REMZI: It made me feel included.

CRAVER: Yeah.

REMZI: Which kid were you, the fat kid?

CRAVER: The tough kid.

REMZI: Of course.

CRAVER: Some of those fuckers were still moving.

REMZI: Right here, where we're sitting, long ago they gave us the zero and the wheel.

CRAVER: Civilians.

REMZI: Irrigation and organized religion and large-scale trade.

CRAVER: But there are no civilians in Iraq.

REMZI: Laws and cities and schools. *(Beat)* That was in 2000 B C.

CRAVER: Bad fucking luck.

REMZI: The first poet known in history.

CRAVER: Those pilots took whatever bombs they could get their hands on, even the clusters and five-hundred-pounders.

REMZI: A woman called Enheduanna.

CRAVER: Imagine dropping a five-hundred-pound bomb on a Volkswagen! Every moving thing. Terminated. Thirty fucking miles of scrap metal, scrap meat. All scrapped. *(He lets out a howl that is half celebration and half terror.)* And I've never seen guys dig that fast. Forty-nine holes.

REMZI: They were going home. We shot them in the back. There are laws regarding warfare.

CRAVER: You're going to get out of the truck this time.

REMZI: I can't.

CRAVER: Yes you can, and I'll make you.

REMZI: Don't ask me to do it, Craver. I'm warning you.

CRAVER: But I have to. Get out of the truck this time and walk along the road with me. Get out of the truck this time and help me. Help me.

REMZI: No.

CRAVER: Someone has to do it.

REMZI: But not you!

CRAVER: Fuck off.

REMZI: What was it like, you son of a bitch? To carry a man's leg?

CRAVER: We were ordered to pick up—

REMZI: *(Interrupts)* To carry a man's leg when the man is no longer attached?

CRAVER: To pick up the pieces and put them in the holes. The dozers covered the pieces we found with sand.

REMZI: Is that what you think we're doing, burying them?

CRAVER: We buried them.

REMZI: We're covering them up. So no one will ever know. I saw you, Craver. I saw you.

CRAVER: It was like a limb of a tree. No. It was like the branch of a tree. That's how heavy it was. I said to myself: Craver, you're not carrying what you think you're carrying. It's just a piece of tree. For the fire. And you're out in your backyard in Hazard, Kentucky, and he's still alive, my father, and my mother still laughs, and we're having a barbecue. And I can smell the coals.

REMZI: One of the bodies I saw...it was very...burned. In one of the vans. For a minute I thought. Well. He looked like.... Maybe it was the sun on my head. I don't know. I put my finger inside his mouth. I wanted to touch him someplace where he wasn't *(Beat)* burned.

CRAVER: Touch me.

REMZI: Every fucking time it tastes different with you. No.

CRAVER: You didn't try and stop it, did you? *(Shouts)* Did you?

(Some moments of silence.)

REMZI: Why are we here *(Beat)* killing Arabs?

CRAVER: For love? Say it's for love. Don't say for oil. Don't say for freedom. Don't say for world power. I'm sick of that. I'm so fucking sick of that. It's true, isnt it? We're here for love. Say it just once. For me.

REMZI: We're here for love.

(They kiss.)

Scene Five

*(*BOXLER *appears with a black box.* LUE MING *stands watching him in the shadows.* BOXLER *speaks to the audience.)*

BOXLER: Trust me. I'm the man with the box. The Amnesty box. And this time I'm in...Iraq. Is that right? *(Beat)* This box you see before you is a very special box. It's a common device we use here within the military, a receptacle in which soldiers can relieve themselves of contraband, no questions asked. Would you like to drop something in it? You can't take those bits and pieces home with you. No, no, no. I've already made the rounds with the other troops. You're not alone. *(Lifts the lid just a bit but then slams it shut)* What distinguishes this particular box is its stench. Now some soldiers are more attached to their souvenirs than others; in one instance, a severed arm was discovered on a military flight leaving the base for Chicago. One might assume that someone somewhere would be disciplined for anatomical trophy-hunting but no, not this time. Lucky, lucky. Are you listening? I'm ready for hell, but they won't have me and that's where they're wrong. *(Beat)* All that nasty shit, it took place all the time, before I even killed my first one. But they weren't interested then. And then when they were, bingo, there I was. *(Beat)* Yes, I did it. I never denied it.

*(*LUE MING *steps forward.)*

LUE MING: March 16, 1968. Charlie Company...

BOXLER: A unit of the America Division's 11th Light Infantry Brigade entered—

LUE MING: Attacked.

BOXLER: Attacked an undefended village on the coast of Central Vietnam and took the lives—

LUE MING: Murdered.

BOXLER: And murdered approximately five hundred old men, women, and children. The killing took place over four hours. Sexual violations...

LUE MING: Rape, sodomy.

BOXLER: Anatomical infractions.

LUE MING: Unimaginable mutilations.

BOXLER: Unimaginable. Yes. By the time I went to trial, public opinion was in my favor. T-shirts, buttons, mugs. One company wanted to put my face on a new cereal.

LUE MING: And my daughter?

BOXLER: It's over now. They say it's over.

LUE MING: The past is never over.

BOXLER: The war is over.

LUE MING: Which one?

BOXLER: Do you have anything you want to put in the box?

LUE MING: Can I take something out?

BOXLER: It's supposed to be a one-way thing.

LUE MING: Give the box to me. Give the box—

BOXLER: *(Interrupts)* I can't do that.

LUE MING: Give the box to me, or I'll hunt you across this desecrated world forever. *(Beat)* You owe me a favor.

(He hands it over to her. She opens the lid and feels about inside. She pulls out her braid.)

LUE MING: It's my braid. My braid!

BOXLER: Can we call it quits?

(LUE MING looks at him but doesn't respond.)

Scene Six

(REMZI and FAIROUZ the night before he leaves for the Mideast. FAIROUZ is tickling him.)

FAIROUZ: I'm going to tickle you until you pee in your pants.

REMZI: Stop it. Get off of me! Stop it!

FAIROUZ: What will the other soldiers say?

(REMZI *wrestles her off and now tickles her.*)

REMZI: You're so jealous. You can't stand me leaving.

FAIROUZ: Let's meet up in the Territories.

REMZI: You'll have to come out of the house!

FAIROUZ: We could look for the village where we might have been born. We could go exploring, find relatives, take photos and—

REMZI: *(Interrupts)* If I get a leave, I'm going to go somewhere...fun. With my buddies. *(Beat)* Hey. But I'll tell you what. I am going to send you back something very special.

FAIROUZ: Send something for Mother, too.

REMZI: Maybe I'll even fall in love over there and bring somebody home with me. They do that in wars. Come back with lovers and wives.

FAIROUZ: If you fall in love, will you let me meét him?

(Some moments of silence)

REMZI: Now you're going to be punished for your foul and lecherous tongue!

(He grabs her foot and begins to tickle it.)

FAIROUZ: Not that one, you fool! I can't feel it.

REMZI: *(Playfully)* Oops. Sorry! *(He grabs her other foot and tickles it.)*

FAIROUZ: Stop it. Stop it! Now go on or you'll miss your bus. *(She kisses him on the cheek to shut him up)* Nothing more. Just go. Go on.

(He exits.)

FAIROUZ: Get out of here!

(LUE MING *appears.* FAIROUZ *talks to her as though she were* REMZI.)

FAIROUZ: No. Wait a minute....It doesn't matter now....We were children then. Are you listening to me? I'm thinking of leaving too, you know. Perhaps I'll make a trip, all on my own. Yes. I might even start a clinic out there, at the edge of the world. You don't believe me? Well, you just wait. When I—

LUE MING: *(Interrupts)* Fairouz. I get leave in a few months. Don't do anything rash. Just wait 'til I get back.

FAIROUZ: Those who wait, burn. *(Knowing now that it is* LUE MING*)* They won't send home the body.

Scene Seven

(FAIROUZ *and* CRAVER *are in his motel room.*)

FAIROUZ: The Army won't send home the body.

CRAVER: What's it matter? It's just a body. It's not him.

(*Split scene:* REMZI *and* BOXLER *elsewhere on stage.* BOXLER *ties* REMZI's *hands and blindfolds him.* LUE MING *stands watching.*)

FAIROUZ: I want to see his body. It belongs to us.

CRAVER: It. It. Just what the fuck are you talking about? He's gone. I don't want anything to do with the it.

(FAIROUZ's *foot hurts her.*)

FAIROUZ: I think I twisted it again.

CRAVER: You should see a doctor. (*Beat*) Let me see.

FAIROUZ: I don't usually show men my foot unless I take my pants off first.

(CRAVER *takes a look at her foot.*)

FAIROUZ: It doesn't smell very good, does it? Remzi used to crush grass, and dandelions, sweet clover, sometimes even the wings of insects, all together in a bowl. He was quite a medic.

LUE MING: (*To* REMZI): Devil's feet, devil's feet, devil's feet.

CRAVER: May I?

FAIROUZ: You want to kiss my foot?

CRAVER: Yes.

REMZI: (*Chants with a deadpan voice*) Fairouz Saboura has devil's feet.

FAIROUZ: Because you want to make it better?

LUE MING: (*Chants*) Dirty Arab devil, you go home!

FAIROUZ: Or because I told you he used to do that?

REMZI: (*Chants*) Dirty Arab devil, you go home!

LUE MING: (*Chants*) Get her shoe. Pull off her shoe.

CRAVER: Both.

REMZI: (*Chants*) Hold her down and pull off her shoe.

CRAVER: For both reasons.

FAIROUZ: All right.

(CRAVER *leans to kiss her foot.*)

REMZI: No!

(FAIROUZ *pulls her foot away from* CRAVER.)

FAIROUZ: Don't.

(REMZI *cannot get loose. He is again "seeing" his sister being beaten.*)

REMZI: Get the fuck off her, you motherfuckers!

FAIROUZ: Remzi!

BOXLER: *(To* REMZI*)* We had an Iraqi prisoner. I stuck the knife in, just below the sternum.

CRAVER: I won't hurt you.

BOXLER: And I slit him all the way down.

REMZI: All of you! Back off!

BOXLER: I pulled his rib cage wide open...

REMZI: Leave her alone!

BOXLER: ...and stood inside his body. I said:

REMZI: Fairouz!

BOXLER: Hey, boys, now I'm really standing in Iraq.

CRAVER: I promise you, I won't hurt you.

(FAIROUZ *lets* CRAVER *kiss her foot, then she kicks him.*)

CRAVER: Bitch.

REMZI: Get away from her!

CRAVER: Fucking...Arab whore.

REMZI: Get away from her. I'm warning you!

FAIROUZ: Take a look, Craver. This isn't a B-52. This isn't a Buff. This is a hammer. I could do to your face what they did to my foot.

CRAVER: Go on then. You fucking gimp. Go on. Do it! Hit me! Hit me, you fucking cunt! Please. *(Drops to his knees)* Please. Hit me.

(*She raises the hammer as if to strike him, but instead she runs the hammer over his cheeks.*)

FAIROUZ: How do you remember him now? (*She presses the face of the hammer to his mouth and moves it sexually*) Like this?

REMZI: No!

CRAVER: *(Pushes the hammer away)* No.

(REMZI *goes "unconscious"*. FAIROUZ *and* CRAVER *are alone.*)

CRAVER: A plague. A flood. An ice age. That's what I expected when it was over and I got back here. An earthquake. Something that would rip this country wide open. Eighty-eight thousand tons of explosives dropped. That country is like a body with every bone inside it broken.

FAIROUZ: How did he die?

CRAVER: Every single bone. We tried. Day after day, but there were too many pieces. We couldn't get them all. Do you know how many pieces make up the human body? Two, three hundred thousand. *(Beat)* Dead. Maybe half of them civilians. We bombed the sewers, the electricity, the water. They'll die in the thousands because of bad water. Just bad water.

FAIROUZ: Give me an answer.

CRAVER: They came for us. Both of us.

FAIROUZ: But you're still alive.

CRAVER: The question here isn't how many feet were between Remzi and I. It could have been thirty feet. Or twenty-five. I think it was more like twenty.

FAIROUZ: Tell me.

CRAVER: I had practiced it with him. I got it down just right. Do you want to see how I walked?

(CRAVER does his "walk" for her as she watches him.)

CRAVER: Are you watching me? *(He continues his "walk".)*

Scene Eight

(BOXLER and LUE MING alone)

BOXLER: I remember you. I think I do. Is that what you want? An apology? Why didn't you just say so? Hey. Really. I'm sincerely sorry. I've always been sorry. Besides, I wasn't completely heartless. You didn't know I shot your kid, because I shot you first.

LUE MING: You said you'd let her live if I did what you wanted. You couldn't get it up. That's why you killed us both.

BOXLER: I had a war on my mind.

LUE MING: What is it like to kill a child?

BOXLER: You're sick.

LUE MING: I have to know.

BOXLER: It's simple: A bit of...a clump of...a piece of... *(Beat)* a piece of the future is alive, and then it isn't.

LUE MING: Were you ever in love?

BOXLER: Oh, yes. Long ago. I was born a human being, you know. But one can't stay that way forever. One has to mature. *(Beat)* Maybe it was you I fell in love with. I mean, it could have happened, couldn't it?

(He kisses her. She does not respond.)

LUE MING: Why wasn't one time enough?

BOXLER: Because I wanted to kiss you again. Naturally.

LUE MING: Why did you have to shoot her twice? Three times? Just to make sure?

BOXLER: Just to make sure, I did it four times. And shooting a child, if you must know, is rather exceptional. It's like shooting an angel. There's something religious about it.

LUE MING: I woke up after you and your troops were gone. I woke up with my child in my arms. A dead child weighs so much more than a live one. I carried her back to the village. When I was well again, I continued my work with the Vietcong. I was one of their top commanders. I searched for you everywhere. Everywhere. With more passion than one would a lost lover. But I never found you.

BOXLER: Just how did you die?

LUE MING: I can't remember. How long have you been dead?

BOXLER: Calley is still alive and well in Georgia, only I've run out on him. I'm his soul. Calley's dead soul.

LUE MING: His soul?

BOXLER: Yes, his soul and I'm homeless.

LUE MING: I don't believe in souls.

BOXLER: Neither do I, but here I am. I go from war to war. It's the only place that feels like home. I didn't kill your daughter. Calley did. I was inside him, looking out, but I didn't do it. I didn't pull the trigger.

LUE MING: You watched.

BOXLER: What else can a soul do but watch? We're not magicians.

LUE MING: Are you suffering?

BOXLER: I can't suffer. I can't, and it hurts me.

LUE MING: Is it terrible?

BOXLER: It tears me apart.

LUE MING: How long will this go on?

BOXLER: World without end.

LUE MING: Delightful. More than I'd hoped. *(Beat)* But I want you to make a sound for me.

(Split scene: FAIROUZ *is watching* REMZI *and* CRAVER, *who do not "see" her watching them.)*

BOXLER: No.

LUE MING: You owe it to me.

FAIROUZ: *(Calls)* Remzi.

BOXLER: I don't know what you're talking about.

FAIROUZ & LUE MING: The sound—

FAIROUZ: ...you made inside you. Not the second time.

LUE MING: Not the third or fourth. But the first time you died.

BOXLER: The first time I died.

LUE MING: Yes.

BOXLER: That would be sometime in November, 1967. There was an old man. He was wounded. He wouldn't have made it anyway. I threw him down a well.

REMZI: *(To* CRAVER) I couldn't say it any louder. I whispered her name. *(Whispers)* Fairouz.

CRAVER: *(Whispers)* Fairouz.

REMZI: There were five of them.

FAIROUZ: Go on.

BOXLER: I threw him down a well. An old man. I heard his head go crack against the stone wall and then splash.

REMZI: One of the boys had just come out of woodshop. He'd been making an end table for his mother for Christmas. He had a hammer.

CRAVER: You were a kid, Remzi.

BOXLER: I was a child once. Did you know that? I liked to run naked and jump up and down on the bed. I had a bath toy. A blue bath toy. I can't remember what it was.

REMZI: They got one of her shoes off. Then the sock. I stood behind the bushes and watched.

CRAVER: You looked out for yourself. That was right.

REMZI: I was afraid that if I tried to stop them they'd do the same to me.

CRAVER: Shhhhhhhhh.

BOXLER: I threw him down the well. I heard a crack. I heard a splash. I heard a crack and a splash, and I died.

CRAVER: You were just a kid.

(CRAVER *and* REMZI *kiss, and* CRAVER *removes* REMZI'*s shirt.*)

FAIROUZ: You were just a child.

BOXLER: When I killed him, I died, though I didn't make a sound when I died. My body just turned and walked back into the village to finish the rest of the job.

LUE MING: But I heard it. I heard the splash. And I heard you die.

FAIROUZ: Do you want to know what it sounds like?

LUE MING: What it sounds like to go on living and the child in your arms is so heavy and she is dead and you are dead and I am dead but—

FAIROUZ: We just keep living.

BOXLER: Forever and ever.

LUE MING: It sounded like this:

(LUE MING, FAIROUZ, *and* BOXLER *all scream "no." Their screams are deafening and mixed with the sound of thundering jets.* REMZI *and* CRAVER *look up at the jets above them, which are awe-inspiring.*)

Scene Nine

(CRAVER *and* FAIROUZ *in his motel room.* CRAVER *is still holding* REMZI'*s shirt.*)

CRAVER: That's beautiful. Sad Eyes. The C B Us were prohibited weapons, like the napalm, cluster, and fragmentation. But Sad Eyes. Who would have had the heart to try and stop a weapon named Sad Eyes? Eyes like his. Not sad, really. But confused. Or furious. Or scared.

(REMZI *appears as a vision.* CRAVER *speaks to him.*)

CRAVER: The first time we made love, we were so scared and I started to cry. It was a first time for both of us, and it hurt. You leaned over me and kissed the back of my neck and you said over and over:

REMZI: You are my white trash, and I love you.

(CRAVER *mouths the words along with* REMZI.)

CRAVER & REMZI: You are my white trash, and I love you.

CRAVER: They caught us together, out behind the barracks. They were lower ranks. Just kids. Like me. Kids who grew up with garbage in their backyards. Kids who never got the summer jobs, who didn't own C D players. They knocked us around. After a while, they took us to a room.

Handed us over to an upper rank. There was a British officer and an Iraqi prisoner in there too, and they were laughing and saying: sandnigger. Indian. Gook. *(Beat)* Remzi. Well. He went wild. He jumped one of those officers. I was standing there. I couldn't move. I couldn't....Then somebody hit me over the head, and I went out. *(Beat)* The first time I came to, the prisoner was down and he kept waving his arms like he was swimming, doing the backstroke, and Remzi was there and I could hear his voice, but it was like trying to see through a sheet of ice. *(Beat)* My head was spinning, and it was snowing stars. In that room. In the middle of the biggest bunch of hottest nowhere in the world and it was snowing stars and Remzi in the center of it and this one officer or maybe it was two and there was a knife and the Iraqi had stopped moving—I think he was dead—and they were all over him and having a good time at it. Like kids in the snow. *(Beat)* Do you want to know how you died, Remzi?

REMZI: Friendly fire.

CRAVER: One of them had his arm around my neck, choking me, while another one held you down. I shouted for you to stay down but you wouldn't stay down. Each time he knocked you down you stood up. He hit you in the mouth so many times I couldn't tell anymore what was your nose and what was your mouth. *(Beat)* What did you call the other soldiers when you first joined up?

REMZI: Family.

CRAVER: When I woke up, I took him in my arms. The blood had stopped coming out. *(Beat)* Five foot...eleven inches. That's how tall you were. I used to run my hand up and down your body like I was reading the bones.

REMZI: I wanted to travel everyplace on your body. Even the places you'd never been. Love can make you feel so changed you think the world is changed. Up 'til then, we'd survived the war.

REMZI: *(To* CRAVER*)* What are you?

FAIROUZ: *(To* CRAVER*)* What are you?

REMZI: *(Louder)* What are you, Craver?

CRAVER: *(Whispers)* What are you? What are you? *(Shouts)* What are you, Craver?

*(*REMZI *says the following words with* CRAVER, *beginning with "Indian."* REMZI*'s words are spoken just a fraction sooner than* CRAVER*'s.)*

CRAVER: I am a White Trash,

CRAVER & REMZI: Indian, Sandnigger, Brown Trash, Arab, Gook Boy, Faggot—

REMZI: *(To* FAIROUZ*)* From the banks of the Kentucky river.

Scene Ten

(REMZI as a vision, as a child, making a "mix" for FAIROUZ's foot. FAIROUZ watches him, as though from a long distance. CRAVER listens from the shadows.)

FAIROUZ: He and I. We were never children. We were pieces of children. After that. But what is a piece of a child?

REMZI: Grass. Black pepper. Gold. From a gold crayon.

FAIROUZ: Sweetness doesn't last. Bitter lasts. Bile lasts. I am looking. Yes. I am looking for him.

REMZI: Pancake syrup. Lots of that.

FAIROUZ: And I don't want to find him. Not now. Not tomorrow. But I'm looking.

(CRAVER exits.)

FAIROUZ: I don't want him to come back to me as him, but as a boy wearing my face. *(Beat)* Where you ended, I began.

REMZI: Ready, Fairouz? *(Calls)* Are you ready? *(To himself)* This one's just right. Won't sting.

FAIROUZ: And the sand. I can't sleep because of it. Everywhere. Inside my pillow. Inside my sleep. I'm walking. Walking and calling for you. But the sand slides below my feet, stopping me, keeping me in place. And the wind throwing handfuls. But then in the distance. I see. Something. Dark. Moving. Moving towards me.

REMZI: Eggshells. Mint.

FAIROUZ: And it seems hours, years until I can see. What. Yes. That it's a child. Five or six. A boy. The wind has torn small pieces from your body. With each step you take towards me you are less whole. When we reach each other, you are almost transparent.

REMZI: It's too dry. *(Calls)* Bring me some water.

FAIROUZ: Almost nothing left. I know I must say your name. Now. But I can't. There's no sand in my mouth. No wind. But I can't say it.

REMZI: *(Calls)* Are you coming?

FAIROUZ: I can't. Say it. And then you're moving away from me, moving back. I open my mouth. To say it. I say: Fairouz.

REMZI: *(Calls)* Fairouz.

FAIROUZ: My own name. Not yours. And, in that moment, the sun drills brilliant through your chest. And then you are. Gone.

Scene Eleven

(CRAVER *and* FAIROUZ *in his motel room.*)

FAIROUZ: The ram's horn. Why did he send me the ram's horn?

CRAVER: He carved your name on the inside. It took him three hours to do it. His sister would have appreciated it. You should have given it to her.

FAIROUZ: I am his sister.

CRAVER: Yes. You are. *(He does a headstand)*

FAIROUZ: Why do you do that?

CRAVER: I'm training my balance.

FAIROUZ: Remzi had no balance.

(CRAVER *comes out of the headstand.*)

CRAVER: No?

FAIROUZ: He said balance could be a bad thing, a trick to keep you in the middle, where things add up, where you can do no harm.

CRAVER: Remzi said that?

FAIROUZ: No. But he might have. *(Beat)* I'll go where ever I need to go. I won't leave them in peace.

CRAVER: Remzi said you were the best sister any brother—

FAIROUZ: *(Interrupts)* Don't. Please. *(Beat)* It's terrible, isn't it? To be freed like this. Are you going to talk?

CRAVER: I'm going to try.

FAIROUZ: But what is it for?

CRAVER: It might keep me alive. Talking about it might keep me alive.

FAIROUZ: I mean the ram's horn. What is it for?

CRAVER: He said.

(REMZI *appears and gets in position to race.*)

REMZI: I want to race.

CRAVER: He said if you blow on it, it will make a noise.

REMZI: I haven't had a good race in almost...

CRAVER: You're on! *(Joins* REMZI. *Gets down in a starting position to run with him)* Motherfucker. Ready?

*(*CRAVER *is in two realities now and speaks to both* REMZI *and* FAIROUZ *with ease.)*

FAIROUZ: A noise.

REMZI: I'm going to beat you this time!

FAIROUZ: All right.

CRAVER: On your mark.

FAIROUZ: Will it be loud?

REMZI: I'm going to pass you by so fast, I'm going to, bang, disappear right in front of you!

CRAVER: *(To* FAIROUZ*)* Fucking loud. *(To* REMZI*)* Get set?

REMZI: You just watch me.

FAIROUZ: Fucking loud. I like that.

REMZI: Just watch me!

FAIROUZ: God damn, fucking loud!

CRAVER & REMZI: Go!

(As the two men move to run, the lights go black.)

END OF PLAY

SELECT BIBLIOGRAPHY

Augustin, Ebba, ed. *Palestinian Women: Identity and Experience.* London and New Jersey: Zed Books, 1993.

Bennis, Phyllis and Moushabeck, Michel, eds. *Beyond the Storm: A Gulf Crisis Reader.* New York: Olive Branch Press, 1991.

Bilton, Michael and Sim, Kevin. *Four Hours in My Lai.* New York: Viking, 1992.

Boyne, Col. Walter. *Weapons of Desert Storm.* Illinois: Signet Special, 1991.

Chomsky, Noam. *The Fateful Triangle: The United States, Israel and the Palestinians.* Boston: South End Press, 1983.

Chomsky, Noam and Herman, Edward S. *Manufacturing Consent: The Political Economy of the Mass Media.* New York: Pantheon Books, 1988.

Clark, Ramsey and Others. *War Crimes: A Report on United States War Crimes Against Iraq.* Washington, D.C.: Maisonneuve Press, 1992.

Cleaver, Richard and Myers, Patricia, eds. *A Certain Terror: Heterosexism, Militarism, Violence and Change.* Chicago: American Friends Service Committee, 1993.

Darwish, Mahmoud. *Music of the Human Flesh: Poems of the Palestinian Struggle.* London: Heinemann, 1980.

Edelman, Bernard. *Letters Home from Vietnam.* New York: W.W. Norton, 1985.

Giannou, Dr. Chris. *Besieged: A Doctor's Story of Life and Death in Beirut.* London: Bloomsbury, 1991.

Gittings, John, ed. *Beyond the Gulf War.* London: CIIR, 1991.

Janz, Wes and Vickie Abrahamson, eds. *War of the Words: The Gulf War Quote by Quote.* Minnesota: Bobbleheads Press, 1991.

Khalidi, Walid, ed. *All That Remains: The Palestinian Villages Occupied and Depopulated by Israel in 1948.* Washington, D.C.: Institute for Palestinian Studies, 1992.

Murphy, Jay. *For Palestine.* New York: Writers and Readers Press, 1993.

Peters, Cynthia, ed. *Collateral Damage: The "New World Order" at Home & Abroad.* Boston: South End Press, 1992.

Said, Edward W. *After the Last Sky: Palestinian Lives.* New York: Pantheon Books, 1986.

Said, Edward W. *Covering Islam: How the Media and the Experts Determine How We See the Rest of the World.* New York: Pantheon Books, 1981.

Shaheen, Jack G. *The T V Arab.* Ohio: Bowling Green State University Press, 1984.

Shilts, Randy. *Conduct Unbecoming: Gays and Lesbians in the U S Military.*

New York: St. Martin's Press, 1993.
Tucker, Judith E., ed. *Arab Women: Old Boundaries, New Frontiers.* Indiana:
Indiana University Press, 1993.
Young, Elise G. *Keepers of History: Women and the Israeli-Palestinian Conflict.*
New York: Teachers College Press, 1992.

Publications

The Guardian (U K)
The Independent (U K)
Lies of Our Times
M.E.R.I.P.
The Nation
The New Statesman and Society
The New York Times
Out Now
Z Magazine

SLAUGHTER CITY

ORIGINAL PRODUCTION

SLAUGHTER CITY had its first performance on 17 January 1996 at the Royal Shakespeare Company. The cast and creative contributors were:

ROACH . . . . Lisa Gaye Dixon
MAGGOT . . . . Sophie Stanton
BRANDON . . . . .Alexis Daniel
COD . . . . .Olwen Fouere
TUCK . . . . .Rudolph Walker
TEXTILE WORKER . . . . Mairead Carty
SAUSAGE MAN . . . . Robert Langdon Lloyd
BAQUIN . . . . Linal Haft

Director . . . . .Ron Daniels
Designer . . . . Ashley Martin-Davies
Lighting . . . . Hugh Vanstone
Sound score . . . . Glyn Perrin
Movement . . . . .Struan Leslie
Fights . . . . .Terry King
Dialect coach . . . . Charmian Hoare
Sound . . . . Monkey and Tony Brand
Company voice work . . . . .Barbara Houseman and Andrew Wade
Stage manager . . . . Michele Enright
Deputy stage manager . . . . Nick Chesterfield
Assistant stage manager . . . . Lucy Bovington

CHARACTERS & SETTING

ROACH, *an African-American worker in her mid-thirties*
MAGGOT, *a white worker in her mid-thirties*
BRANDON, *a white worker in his early twenties*
COD, *a white worker of Irish descent, mid-thirties*
TUCK, *an African-American, mid-forties*
TEXTILE WORKER, *a woman in her twenties*
SAUSAGE MAN, *a white man, somewhat elderly, energetic*
BAQUIN, *a white company manager in his fifties*

TIME

Now and then

PLACE

Slaughter City, U S A

SET

Should be minimal and not "realistic"

I came to the cities in a time of disorder
When hunger ruled.
I came among men in a time of uprising
And I revolted with them.
So the time passed away
Which on earth was given me.

I ate my food between massacres.
The shadow of murder lay upon my sleep.
And when I loved, I loved with indifference.
I looked upon nature with impatience.
So the time passed away
Which on earth was given me.

In my time streets led to the quicksand.
Speech betrayed me to the slaughterer.
There was little I could do. But without me
The rulers would have been more secure. This was my hope.

"To Those Born Later" Bertolt Brecht

ACT ONE

Prelude

(The stage is empty but for a woman textile worker, her back to us, working over her cloth. She speaks as if in a trance. COD is elsewhere on stage, watching her work. We are in a textile factory setting, "somewhere" in the past)

TEXTILE WORKER: Pull the cloth, punch it down, cut three out, and trace. Hurry, hurry, don't slow down, keep your cheer and grace.

COD: Could you look up for a second? Hey.

TEXTILE WORKER: Pull the cloth, punch it down, cut three out, and trace.

COD: *(Calls)* Is anybody out there?

TEXTILE WORKER: Hurry, hurry, don't slow down, keep your cheer and grace.

COD: The doors are locked. *(To TEXTILE WORKER)* I'm talking to you.

TEXTILE WORKER: When I day dream, my hands sweep the cloth—

COD: What floor are we on?

TEXTILE WORKER: —like water over the keys of a piano.

(We hear the distorted sound of a siren in the distance)

COD: We've got to get out of here.

TEXTILE WORKER: *(She touches his face gently)* Oh, what eyes you have. Black eyes. Like my eyes.

COD: I haven't got any eyes. I'm not even born yet.

(The woman turns back to her cloth to work. Transfixed, COD watches her.)

(End Prelude)

Scene One

(Lights up on MAGGOT, ROACH, and BRANDON working. They are hosing down the heads of carcasses which are suspended above them, and slicing off bits of gristle from the bone. When the workers work, the feeling should be one of the intensity of industrial labor here on earth and perhaps also in hell.)

ROACH: Maggot? *(No answer)* Maggot? Come on, sweetie. I said I was sorry. It was just a joke, wasn't it, Brandon?

BRANDON: A masterstroke, an okeydoke joke.

MAGGOT: A just plain you haven't-got-any-brains-left-for-God-to-suck-out-of-your-skull joke.

ROACH: Did you eat it?

BRANDON: Didn't even pause 'til she got to the claws.

ROACH: Maggot? Come on.

MAGGOT: Not unless you buy me three packs of brand name smokes and on third shift you snap guts and let me scale.

ROACH: You know I won't snap guts.

MAGGOT: I've been snappin' guts since I was seventeen.

BRANDON: Princess of Excrementis.

MAGGOT: Just because I turned you down three years ago for a Dairy Queen date...

BRANDON: That was before I realized that what you need is a dull blade, baby, a blade that won't cut meat.

(Double bell sounds, which means a short break for the workers. At the moment the horn sounds, all work/assembly line movement stops. MAGGOT flexes her hands, which are hurting her.)

ROACH: Two packs of generics, and I'll go third shift on the night you want off, 'cept Saturday—

BRANDON: *(Interrupts)* Hey! Here it comes: I'm startin' to itch.

(COD enters, headed for the kill floor. He is a slim, young Irishman, who is stronger than he looks. BRANDON jumps in front of COD and pretends to sword fight.)

BRANDON: Unsheathe from your scabbard, you scoundrel, you fleabane, you scabrous snake.

(COD does not respond.)

BRANDON: Look at this, ladies. Not a peep. Why, they're no fun, these bacterial spots. And, Lord, how they—

MAGGOT & ROACH: Itch, itch, itch.

BRANDON: *(Like a commercial)* Are you covered with raised, roughened, or unwholesome patches?

MAGGOT & ROACH: Scratch, scratch, scratch.

BRANDON: Do you sometimes feel a little down, like a crust of hard blood and serum over a wound?

(The three workers circle COD.)

MAGGOT & ROACH: *(Together)* Are you characterized by crustaceous spots?

BRANDON: Then you need Local 226.

MAGGOT: Only Local 226—

ROACH, MAGGOT, & BRANDON: Don't need you.

(They stand in a circle around COD.)

ROACH: You know what Scab stands for?

MAGGOT, BRANDON, & ROACH: Stupid Cunts And Bastards.

(COD *spits on the ground at their feet.)*

ROACH: *(Speaks)* It's raining, it's pouring

MAGGOT & ROACH: *(Together)* The scab's gone a-whoring!

MAGGOT: Watch you don't bump your head.

BRANDON: Or you won't be back in the morning!

(MAGGOT *begins to steel her knife, the others do the same.* ROACH *hums a tune and then the three workers sing the following. When one of them sings, the others hum.)*

BRANDON: I'm gonna cut you, Scabby, gonna cut you deep
with my sweet, blue kisses, gonna send you off to sleep.

MAGGOT: I'm gonna slice you, sweetheart, gonna slice you wide—

ROACH: —with my hot, fast lips I'm gonna take you for a ride.

(Bell sounds again. The workers move back to their job. COD *stands silently, watching them.)*

(End Scene One)

Scene Two

(BAQUIN *in his office, with* TUCK, *a supervisor)*

TUCK: Mood. The mood?

BAQUIN: Yes. What's the mooood in the packhouse?

TUCK: Sickly. Yeah, a sickly mood in there.

BAQUIN: Well, their boycott of our products has put a dent in our sales,
but a dent is a dent. We can survive a dent. What we need is a mooooove.
(Clears his throat) A turn in the right direction. Some better weather.
What do you say we...What's your name again?

TUCK: Tuck. Supervisor Tuck.

BAQUIN: Yes, well, fellows come and go here. Mostly Affirmative Action types. They don't always last—

TUCK: *(Interrupts)* Affirmative action didn't get this job for me.

BAQUIN: I didn't mean to imply. No. Not you. But then, why you? What makes Buck special?

TUCK: I started on the kill floor, sir. About fifteen years ago. I worked my way up. Now I take night classes at Bellarmin. Just about got my degree.

BAQUIN: Where do you see yourself in five years?

TUCK: Do you like your job?

BAQUIN: Clever! Very clever.

TUCK: Yeah. But I've also been cut. *(He shows his arm.)* Sliced. *(He shows his torso.)* And hacked. *(He shows where a finger is maimed.)*

BAQUIN: Now, don't get sentimental. We've got a business to run. Special interests are slicing our hearts, gutting innovation, shredding our ability to compete—

TUCK: You've got two Mercedes.

BAQUIN: That's what I mean. Fellow that runs I B P's got three. *(Laughs)*

TUCK: They won't go easy for the mechanical sharpener, and seniority rights are still top of the list.

BAQUIN: Seniority rights. I need capable workers. A worker is like a nose. It runs good, runs on time. But like all things, it gets stuffed. You pick it. It gets stuffed again. It starts costing too much to pick. What do you expect me to do? Be their grandmother and carry out their snot rags in their old age?

TUCK: I would get rid of some trouble makers.

BAQUIN: I've done that.

TUCK: There are some more.

BAQUIN: Tell me something, son, I heard a rumor the other day that some of our boys in the packhouse aren't circumcised. The Board doesn't like it. It's not good for packhouse reputation. *(Beat)* What about you?

(No answer from TUCK*)*

BAQUIN: Well, if you're not, you should go get it done. Those little hats collect dirt. And you don't seem like the kind of man to collect dirt.

TUCK: No...

BAQUIN: What we need is to raise the spirits around here. We need to give the union the feeling that it has a voice. That the boss listens. That we're a team.

TUCK: They want a new contract and a guaranteed pace.

BAQUIN: That's not a team concept. Let's start a reading circle. Management will supply the books. We'll discuss literature. Start with Thomas Hardy. *(Beat)* What about an environmental program? We could get a committee together to discuss *Partula affinis*. *(He holds up a glass bowl.)* It's the only current member of a small and exclusive club of species that have been wiped out by man.

TUCK: What is it?

BAQUIN: A snail.

TUCK: Looks like snot.

BAQUIN: It's the last single snail of its kind. I bought it from the University of Virginia. Under-the-table deal. They get our sliced meats thirty percent off. It's a hermaphrodite, this one. If it wants to, it can mate with itself. When this small mollusc dies, its species will enter the eternal night of extinction. Hard to imagine, isn't it? *(Beat)* Do you think we could stir up some interest? An after-work hobby?

TUCK: They're pretty tired when they get off work.

BAQUIN: Imagine. The ultimate loneliness. To be the last of your kind. *(Beat)* Who's that kid, the one always sparking trouble over the knives? College kid. Full of spunk.

TUCK: Brandon.

BAQUIN: Find a reason to fire him.

TUCK: He's one of our best with a knife.

BAQUIN: Then promote him. That should turn him around.

TUCK: By the way, he's back. The guy with a sausage grinder, old hand-held thing. Nasty. He's waiting in the hall to see you. He won't leave. Says he started the company.

BAQUIN: Nonsense. No one started this company. It's been here since... the beginning of time. *(Beat)* Now, give me a check on their..on their... mooooood again. *(Clears his throat)* At the end of the week.

TUCK: I'll do that, Mr Baquin.

BAQUIN: That a boy, Buck.

(TUCK exits. BAQUIN sits at his desk and clears his throat again and speaks aloud, though he is alone.)

BAQUIN: At the end of the week. Give me a report on their... *(He looks around him, in some distress. He tries again.)* At the end of the week. Give me a report on their...general well-being.

(End Scene Two)

Scene Three

(BRANDON *is showing* ROACH *how to pull loins, one of the toughest jobs in the industry.*)

BRANDON: Reach and pull. Reach and pull. Got it? *(Beat)* Half the men I know can't pull loins.

ROACH: For a number one pay bracket a whole week, I'm damn sure gonna try.

BRANDON: Now, you got seven to nine coming at you a minute. When the horn goes for the speed up, you get up to twelve.

(He puts his hands on hers to show her. She pulls away.)

ROACH: Just show me, O K?

BRANDON: The important thing is you've got to dip your knife before each cut. Like this. And swing the blade out over the loin like this. You have to be quick. Real quick.

ROACH: I got it.

(They pull loins side by side)

BRANDON: You've got...nice, quick arms.

ROACH: Why don't you go on back to college where you belong?

BRANDON: 'Cause I like the pay.

ROACH: That's the difference between you and me, besides the color: You like the pay. I need it.

BRANDON: When I started working here, I vomited every Monday morning. They dropped me down on the kill floor pulling black guts, cleaning chitterlings. Hog shit in my nose, in my mouth, all day long. Then I was trimming jaw bones. Lost half a thumb, see? Moving up. Moving up in the pay bracket. Ten cents more. Fifteen cents more. All the time waiting to get to the knives. Then I was head boner. Slipped a disk twice. Twenty-five cents more. Then moving up again to a scalder. Forty cents. Then forty-five. Hot. That was too damn hot. Then I was bung dropper. Too fucking intimate, cutting the assholes out of hogs. One guy slipped his bung and cut my left thigh to the bone. Then I was splitter. Top rate bracket. Bingo. New used car. Two-bedroom apartment, one for me, one for my television. I like it. I like the money.

ROACH: You like the money. We're making less now at the top pay bracket than we were at the lowest ten years ago.

BRANDON: But that's gonna change for me, cause I'm moving up to formal combat with the meat, straight into that neat, clean seat in the sky.

ROACH: You don't give a damn about the contract, do you?

BRANDON: Sure I do. While I'm here. I'm not budging on knife-sharpening time. The twenty minutes we got now isn't enough.

ROACH: It's about more than knives.

BRANDON: Not to me. What they want is to hire some distempered dildo who doesn't know that one knife is as different from another as two women are different. And this guy is gonna sharpen my knife for me? That fatuous ferret will fold that edge over without even knowing it, and I'll have to break my back all day long cutting with a dull knife.

ROACH: Seniority is the priority.

BRANDON: You never used a loin knife 'til now. Look. The edge of a knife is like a thin piece of hair. What the steel does is it stands it up, so if you angle that steel wrong, you're going to fold that edge over.

ROACH: Hmmm.

(Bell sounds for the break)

BRANDON: I was thinking maybe you *(Beat)* and me, we could take a stroll. Nothing too fancy, a twirl through the park, a couple of cartwheels cross the Belvedere?

ROACH: I already said no. I'm fifteen years older than you.

BRANDON: Maybe you don't dote on white boys.

ROACH: I don't dote on boys period.

BRANDON: You're caught up on this color thing.

ROACH: Since the day I was born.

BRANDON: Well, get over it, Roach. Cast it behind you.

ROACH: Just scale it off me like a fish. Right. Why are you here? Why don't you toddle on back to the U and get some more of that financial aid. Though I doubt you'll learn to figure this side of the fence even if you sit bare-assed on the barbed wire.

BRANDON: Light the candles. It's gonna be another pity party! And guess who gets the gifts? *(Chants)*
'Cause I'm a little white boy,
and the world's my wind-up toy.
I'm the power of the nation.
I'm the source of all creation!

ROACH: *(Double bell sounds for a break. She looks at her watch.)* Isn't it about time you changed your diapers?

BRANDON: Every day I wake up, and people like you are telling me that the world's a rabbit in my hat, right? That I'm the boss. I can't even get my fuckin' knife sharpened the way I want to. Feel this one they did on the machine.

(He takes her hand to make her feel it. She pulls away.)

ROACH: Don't touch people who don't want to be touched.

BRANDON: Tell me something. Who got to you first and ruined it for me?

(Calmly, ROACH *slaps him.)*

BRANDON: If you can keep up *(Beat)* I'll steel your knife for you.

*(*ROACH *doesn't respond.)*

BRANDON: At least until you get the hang of it.

ROACH: And what, Mr Nice Guy, do I have to do in return?

BRANDON: Like ice cream?

ROACH: Depends.

BRANDON: On what?

ROACH: On the cone.

BRANDON: When I said I liked... It wasn't a line. Your arms. They're *(Beat)* stalwart and sturdy.

ROACH: They get the job done.

BRANDON: I like to eat mine out of a cup.

(End Scene Three)

Scene Four

(Supervisor TUCK *stands watching* COD *sweep/mop up offal.)*

TUCK: It's an odd name. Cod. Know what it means?

COD: No.

TUCK: Look it up. I did. It's a fish. From the cold North Atlantic. *(Beat)* Not too bad here, is it? Though I never liked hogs myself. Small eyes.

COD: That transfer you mentioned? I'd rather stay in one place.

TUCK: In Latin your name is *Gadus morrhua*. Don't you think "Gadus" has just a bit more status to it? And status might be what a guy like you needs, Gadus. Gadus?

COD: Yeah.

TUCK: You missed a bit. To your left. *(Beat)* Did you know you were once thought of as a nigger, Gadus? Now don't take offense. I know white folks don't like being called nigger. It gets them confused. *(Beat)* Why are you making those puny strokes. Watch me. *(He takes the broom/mop and makes some masterful and fancy sweeps with it)* History, Gadus. You ever read? That's where you'll find the key. When you Irishmen came over here in the 1800s, after that British potato problem, you were called a dark race, low-browed and savage.

(TUCK gives COD back the broom/mop.)

TUCK: Oh, yeah. You were more feared than us blacks. You were the Celtic Beast, and you chased the women and raped the chickens. That's a fact. You lived side by side us in the slums. Chums we were, you and me. Chummed up and slumming it together. Then you were given a raise. That raise was the right to call us nigger and the right not be called a nigger yourself. So you see, whiteness don't have to be a color, Gadus. It can be a wage. *(Watching him mop)* That's it. Use your shoulders. Pull and push. Pull and push.

COD: The kill floor. I like it there.

TUCK: We'll see. We need you where we need you. *(Beat)* Hold your head up. Don't stoop. A man like you shouldn't stoop. Gadus?

COD: It's just that you're standing in the way and I can't get to it.

(TUCK doesn't move.)

TUCK: Do you dream, Gadus? I dream. But a dream is like the waves a fly makes struggling on the surface of the water. When the fly stops struggling, so does the dream. *(Beat)* Gadus? You're all wet.

COD: It's the heat, sir.

TUCK: It's only seventy in here.

COD: It's hotter than that.

TUCK: Push and pull, Gadus. Push and pull.

(End Scene Four)

Scene Five

(MAGGOT and ROACH are trimming ham bones.)

ROACH: A scab's a scab.

MAGGOT: That doesn't mean he don't have a cute ass.

ROACH: It's scab ass, honey. And that sort of ass never changes its spots. You just like the underdogs. You ever been with someone with a nice colored ass?

MAGGOT: I was with a French guy once.

ROACH: French is white. *(Beat)* A lot of the scabs they brought in here were black. When we said we'd come back to our jobs without a contract, they fired most of those scabs. Just trash. *Black* trash. *(Beat)* I see our boys with their Local 226 T-shirts on, and they are calling them scabs everything they can think of but racial. Cause it's not allowed. Cause we are above that. But I can hear that word behind our white boy's teeth: *(Whispers)* Nigger. Nigger. *(Beat)* That word ever get stuck up behind your teeth, Maggot? When you're cursin and yellin' at those scabs and you're madder than hell, you ever feel that word on your tongue?

MAGGOT: How long have we been best friends, Roach?

ROACH: If promotion time comes, who are they gonna promote, you or me?

MAGGOT: Neither of us is gonna get promoted.

(A light flashes. This signals a speed up. We see the workers work faster.)

ROACH: They're not supposed to speed up 'til after lunch.

MAGGOT: You ever done it with a white man?

ROACH: How white are we talking?

MAGGOT: Ice white.

ROACH: I'm going up to Green River this weekend.

MAGGOT: You won't sleep with a man because he's white!?

ROACH: I got a new set of spinners, yellow tails. Want to come?

MAGGOT: Got no money for gas.

ROACH: Shhh. Look who's coming for supper.

(COD enters with huge meat hooks and chains. He wipes them down and stacks/hangs them.)

ROACH: Aren't you in the smoke department this week?

COD: Injecto pump's down.

MAGGOT: You look like a nice, young man. Where did you find it in that puny little soul of yours to cross our picket line when we were out on strike? Give me a straight answer.

COD: *(The following dialogue is fired back and forth rapidly.)* I have kids to feed.

MAGGOT: Not with our jobs.

COD: It's not your job if you're out there.

MAGGOT: All they want to do is use you like a piece of junk.

COD: Where are you gonna work where they aren't gonna treat you like a piece of junk?

ROACH: Come back on that one, Maggot. We need a come-back.

(MAGGOT *is silent.*)

ROACH: Two points for the scab!

COD: You two talk this bold to the company?

MAGGOT: We haven't got a new contract 'cause low-lifes like you crossed the picket line.

COD: I haven't got any kids.

ROACH: Always sounds better when you bring in the kids.

COD: I want to join your local.

MAGGOT: You can't join a local once you cross their pickets.

ROACH: Trying to change his spots.

COD: A man can have a change of heart, can't he?

ROACH: You're no man, Spotty, and you'll never be part of this union.

COD: I used to be union. A foundry worker. Long time ago... No. A miner. Harlen County...Kentucky... No... That's not right. It was the...yeah...the Colorado coal strike. A few years back.

ROACH: Wait a minute—

MAGGOT: So sometimes you're union and sometimes you're scab?

ROACH: The Colorado Coal Strike. That was in 1914—

COD: *(Interrupts)* You know, the guy whose job I took stands outside the packhouse, all day, uptight, calls me a meat-fucking scab. At 5 a.m. when I walk in, I look the other way. I've never touched a hog alive. Here, I touch them in pieces. I stroke them from the inside out, where they're wet; it's not right.

MAGGOT: Oh, my. What a big mouth you have, Granny!

(MAGGOT *kisses* COD *on the mouth. He doesn't respond. She kisses him again. This time he responds and pushes her away violently.*)

COD: I didn't choose this place. You understand that? It chose me.

(COD *exits as the women watch him in silence.*)

(*End Scene Five*)

Scene Six

(The packinghouse is dark and empty. We see a figure wandering alone, and carefully looking over the packhouse. He is turning what looks like a small musical organ but it's a hand grinder for sausages that is hung about his neck. He speaks to the space around him. He has a German accent.)

SAUSAGE MAN: I came across the ocean, from Zweibrucken, in the late 1800s. I ground meat in my own backyard. I didn't have a pot to piss in. Sausages. I made sausages. All the little bits of bone and gut and cartilage that the rest of the world threw away, I made into something useful. Something edible. And I wrote the song. The sausage song. I wrote the lullaby that rocked this city to sleep:
(Sings) Fischer's, the Sausage Makin' People,
Makes it fun to be hungry.
With my two hands I created an empire out of a single sausage. And I fed you. I fed you! And what do I get in return? No one is happy making my sausages anymore. But still I grind and grind. I fill the skins with meat. I make it fun to be hungry. *(He grinds his grinder faster.)* Ah, what a sound. The sound of hundreds, thousands of sausages filling up the empty spaces in the world. Sausages filling up the empty spaces in our very souls. I love that sound. Like the world in my hands. Like the world going to pieces in my hands.

(End Scene Six)

Scene Seven

(BRANDON, ROACH, and MAGGOT working at metal tables.)

BRANDON: I don't trust him. He's fractious.

MAGGOT: The man's got passion.

ROACH: Only for himself.

MAGGOT: If we strike again, he'll join us.

ROACH: If we strike again, the replacements will turn their backs.

BRANDON: *(To MAGGOT)* You really want to stick your neck out for this yokel?

ROACH: He won't be a part of my union. What's left of it.

MAGGOT: You're a tightass, Roach.

ROACH: Yeah? He's a scab and you're an itch and if you two get to scratching someone is gonna bleed.

MAGGOT: You wouldn't know an itch if it crawled up your leg and bit you.

ROACH: An itch is something a dog gets.

(MAGGOT *barks like a dog, then she picks up a piece of meat and takes a bite out of it.*)

ROACH: You white girls are disgusting. You take a joke so far it'll kill you.

BRANDON: *(To* ROACH, *to interrupt the women)* So...when are you gonna succumb to my sugar cone, baby?

ROACH: You're making me nauseous.

BRANDON: "I find my heart inside my ribs aroused by your impertinence."

MAGGOT: Brandon.

BRANDON: Homer.

MAGGOT: Give it up.

BRANDON: *(To* ROACH) Come on, darlin', I'm hankering. I'm baffled and balked. Just give me half a wink.

ROACH: What a charmer!

MAGGOT: Could charm the shit out of a dead rabbit's ass.

BRANDON: Not much up top, Maggot, and less down below. For a fruit tramp baby, you're a seedy specimen.

MAGGOT: Listen, little man. You don't, can't, won't ever get me hot, 'cause I got a clit the size of a small rodent and I'd just snap you in half like a corn-nut.

ROACH: *(To* BRANDON) If we vote on letting him join, will you back me up with a negative?

BRANDON: I'll back up, bend down and roll up just as far as you want me to. Well?

ROACH: I'll go for a Coke with you, Brandon. A Coke. For an hour.

MAGGOT: Look who's using the itch.

ROACH: But I'm not gonna let you watch me sip it.

BRANDON: Why not? I want to see you sip it. I want to watch that liquid ascend through the straw, up into your moist and marvelous...Fuck! *(He's cut himself on his knife.)* Look at that! Look at that, god damn it. Just try it, he says. Just try it. Machine gives it a good edge. Fuck his edge. *(Shouts to someone offstage)* Fuck your edge. *(Beat)* They're going to replace us. Then they won't need the top-rate knife boys. The mechanical will do it.

ROACH: You better check that at the clinic.

BRANDON: And a mechanical won't ask for a raise. Well, we'll see about that. *(Shouts to offstage)* We'll see about that! One more time and you won't have any knives left to steel. *(He is furious now and drops to his knees and begins hacking at the floor until the knife is ruined. He throws it aside. Silence. Then he speaks quietly.)* That'll fuck your edge.

(End Scene Seven)

Scene Eight

(BAQUIN and TUCK giving the SAUSAGE MAN a tour of the facilities)

BAQUIN: Ah, Baquin's the name, meat's the game. And you are...?

SAUSAGE MAN: I make sausages.

BAQUIN: Ah. Hobby perhaps, or old-style deli? Well, you've come to the right place to see how slaughtering and packing are properly done. *(Meaning the packhouse)* So, what do you think?

SAUSAGE MAN: It makes me sad.

BAQUIN: Ah yes. I know. Do you think I haven't spared a thought for the cow, trembling at that final moment, those big, brown eyes?

SAUSAGE MAN: It's not the cows, dear sir.

BAQUIN: Oh, the pigs...well, the toys are cute but the real thing.... Just think of that book about the pigs who take over the farm...um...Tuck?

TUCK: *Animal Farm*, Mr Baquin. Napoleon and—

BAQUIN: *(Interrupts)* Right! A great writer, Joyce. If we gave pigs—and I'm sure the cows would be right behind them—if we gave them their declaration of rights...Well, who knows, we might all end up as sausages!

SAUSAGE MAN: The workers, the shop-floor, the union...

BAQUIN: They love our sausages!

SAUSAGE MAN: I'm troubled. Deeply troubled. Too much talk and idleness. Kid-gloves, cowardly tactics. Not how we used to do it. Those times then are here, now. I know the rules. I can say yes, no, stay, go. Open, close and fire! And this Company? Ah, if I had ulcers, they'd be the size of oranges by now. Look at you!

(BAQUIN inspects himself.)

SAUSAGE MAN: You're not even triple stitched. I bet you let your socks wear thin before you throw them out!

TUCK: Should I get rid of...?

BAQUIN: P R, Tuck. P R.

SAUSAGE MAN: What we need is to kindle a spark, ignite a little imagination around here. Have you ever felt your blood boil? It's extraordinary.

BAQUIN: I eat lots of bran. Keeps my stress level under control.

SAUSAGE MAN: There's too much sympathy nowadays.

BAQUIN: For the cows? The workers? The pigs?

SAUSAGE MAN: It was different; it used to be an iron-clad operation, lock, stock, and barrel. It's a shame.

BAQUIN: *(Without a clue)* I know what you mean.

SAUSAGE MAN: It saddens me.

BAQUIN: I, too, am deeply touched. Nevertheless, I think you're a bit out of date. If you want to start a competitive business, you—

SAUSAGE MAN: *(Interrupts)* Out of date? I'm your future.

BAQUIN: What?

SAUSAGE MAN: Oh, I'm having no fun at all. Something must be done.

BAQUIN: I agree completely, Mr...?

SAUSAGE MAN: I made the finest sausage links...

BAQUIN: *(Overlapping so that only "links" is clearly defined)* Mr Links, you know, it's an age-old conundrum with us in the meat-packing business: Where does our sympathy go? I confess, I try to steer clear of those big, brown innocent eyes—but man cannot live by greens alone. It thins the blood.

(SAUSAGE MAN is leaving. BAQUIN follows him.)

BAQUIN: Age-old, I confess, yes, and we run a tight ship here and the hands, well, we can't let sympathy out and about or the cows and the pigs, Napoleon—right, Tuck?—well, they'd be ruling the roast...the roost... And be sure to pick up some literature on your way out, we're the professionals.

(SAUSAGE MAN is "gone".)

BAQUIN: Ah, the muddled Old School. Never get a business off the ground these days.

(End Scene Eight)

Scene Nine

(BRANDON alone after everyone has gone home. A makeshift, bloody bandage on his hand, he stands on a work scaffold, then jumps down and clears the space for his "dance." He places his cassette player in the center of the space and then begins to run, jump, and dance around the stage. The feeling is one of a body taking complete

control over the space around it. There is a part of a wrapped carcass hanging from the ceiling. BRANDON cuts it loose with his knife and it falls. He turns off the music to begin the second part of his "show." He circles the carcass, then takes off his shirt and speaks. All this should be stylized. BRANDON has done this sort of "show" before.)

BRANDON: "Let sorrow split my heart— *(He slashes the wrapper open to expose the meat.)* —if ever I did hate thee." *(He gently undresses the carcass and speaks to it.)*
(Sings) I got a mouth like a spider
and a web for you I'll spin.
Just open up a little wider,
with my spinneret, I'm comin' in.
(He throws away the knife and begins to kiss and nip at the carcass. He then holds out his arms.) See the light comin' off my feathers, Love? See it? I'm an angel, and I'm gonna reach my wing so far inside you, I'm going to disappear.

(He pushes his hand, then his arm, inside the carcass. This should be both sensual and frightening. ROACH picks up the knife. She comes up behind him, takes him by the hair and holds the knife to his throat. She is in complete control.)

ROACH: Oh, but that's not enough, my cherub. No. This piece of meat wants your sweet face inside her, your whole head inside her.

(She crushes his face into the carcass, then turns him on his back so she's straddling him, knife still at his throat.)

ROACH: You like this dream, lover boy? What happens in the end? Does she come like he needs her to, like a train, blasting off, straight up to the sky?

BRANDON: He'll never know cause, 'she doesn't want him.

ROACH: This is a sad picture if this is how you want me. In case you haven't heard, we don't like to be cut when we come.

BRANDON: I fuckin' hate you, Roach. I fuckin' hate you, 'cause I want you so bad it's like a knife up my ass.

ROACH: If I could I'd turn it, college boy.

BRANDON: Tuck is gonna promote me.

ROACH: Promote you?

BRANDON: Office work.

ROACH: You've only been here a couple of years.

BRANDON: They want me off the kill floor.

ROACH: Always the fuckin' white boys get promoted.

BRANDON: I can talk, Roach. Hear how I can talk? I pick up words, all kind of words, big words, small words. I pick up words like a dog picks up fleas.

(Beat) But I can't read. How am I going do office work when I can't read? *(Beat)* Shit. My face hurts. Damn it.

ROACH: *(She touches his forehead.)* You've got a fever.

BRANDON: Keep your hand there.

ROACH: You got to get to the hospital. You got blood poisoning.

BRANDON: You're poisoning me.

ROACH: Right. Come on. Get up.

(She helps him to his feet.)

BRANDON: I'm twenty-two years old. I've never been with a woman.

ROACH: What are you saying?

BRANDON: Look at my mouth.

ROACH: So?

BRANDON: No. Look at it. The white marks. Like a halo around my mouth.

ROACH: Pretty.

BRANDON: I quit going to school when I was fifteen, 'cause the words were upside down. Somersaulting. I couldn't keep them in line. I left home and went and lived with my boss. He let me have a corner in his garage. He owned a chain of jewelry stores. I swept, stacked, cooked. One day I dropped a box with some china in it. He hit me until I passed out. When I came to, he was sitting beside me. He had a lure box with him. He said I'd cursed him. I couldn't remember, up 'til then I'd never said a thing but "Yes, sir". He said he'd make sure I never spoke against him again. He took some fish line and a hook out of his box and he sewed my mouth shut. That's why I never could kiss a girl. Because it's always bleeding where the line went through. How can you kiss a girl when your mouth is always bleeding?

ROACH: Your mouth isn't bleeding.

BRANDON: Yeah, it is. I can taste it.

ROACH: There's no blood on your mouth.

BRANDON: Every day I can taste it.

(End Scene Nine)

Scene Ten

(COD is soapboxing the workers as they clean up as they work. The workers laugh at COD; they think he's ridiculous. BRANDON is somewhat crazed with fever.)

COD: What we need around here is some direct action. Shall I tell you what direct action means?

BRANDON: Go to hell...

COD: The worker on the job shall tell the boss when and where the worker shall work—

MAGGOT: Not again. Christ.

COD: —how long, and for what wages and under what conditions.

ROACH: This is gettin' tedious.

COD: The working class and the employer class have nothing in common? I W W? Industrial Workers of the World? *(Beat)* O K. How many of you don't have arthritis from workin' the cold and wet? Maggot? You've got carpal tunnel in both your hands.

MAGGOT: Been operated on twice.

COD: Roach? Back so bad from lifting you got to roll out of bed in the morning?

ROACH: Why do you think we went on strike to begin with?

COD: How about you, Brandon? So tired after a split-double, chasin' half-crazed steers at midnight you just can't get that erection you need for Saturday night?

BRANDON: Fuck your dog, your cat, and any other carnivorous animals you own.

COD: Fucking? Well. Yes. Now, fucking is a key, no matter with who or where or how, and each time a worker fucks in this world, the possibility for their taking power increases, just a little.

MAGGOT: Oh, Scabby's talking dirty!

COD: Because coming is the body's way of saying fuck you to the rules and regulations.

BRANDON: Fuck you.

COD: *(Continuing)* It's catching! Fuck you to the bowing and scraping we live by just to eat. When a worker comes, when we come, it's our body's way of saying: "I am radiant and I am fearless and I will not be disposed of; I am not a piece of meat."

(COD has got their attention now.)

COD: Whatever we win or lose, here is what meat workers will have to accept all over the country, at Swift, Armour, I B P, Hormel.
(Sings) So fold up your arms and sit where you stand
They're gonna hear us across the land

BRANDON: So you like to soap box?

COD: We're sick of getting nothing but an ear of shit
This time it's enough and we say quit.

BRANDON: A little exhibition to flaunt your wares?

COD: We have a world to win.

BRANDON: Could be a world to lose. But since you like to play, let's play.
A little game. You and me. You believe all it takes is to sing a few words
and the boss is going to hand you the plate? All right. Show me some
fortitude. Make me afraid.

COD: Sorry about that office job, Brandie. I know you were counting on it.

BRANDON: Lovely touch. And precise. But let's get back to the matter at
hand. Let's say I'm running this packhouse. I'm running this whole joke.
(He tears off his apron and throws it aside.)

MAGGOT: Sup's got two warnings on your file, Brandon.

BRANDON: And I'm clean. I haven't been standing in blood all day. No gut
in my hair. Hands don't shake. My back is straight. Mouth tastes like I just
brushed my teeth. Nice. But here you are. Just your average guy, cutting
out hog asshole fifteen hours a day, piss running through your veins, gums
swimming in steer blood.

ROACH: Strike three, and there won't be nothing the union can do for you
anymore.

BRANDON: No. How about a bitch. Can you play a bitch? I bet you can.
And I'm the boss. *(He takes up a knife.)* Now, convince me.

*(BRANDON struts about like a "boss." Then he turns on COD. Through most of the
scene the women are mesmerized. They are watching themselves in COD. They are
silent and motionless.)*

BRANDON: That's all very well said, young woman: "Nothing in common,"
but we have everything in common. I need you to do work, and you need
me to have work. We're linked, from birth until death. Star-crossed lovers
igniting in the dark. *(Beat)* Oh dear, your apron's loose. Let's just give it a
little tuck.

(He runs the knife up and down COD's body, sensually)

BRANDON: You like it here, princess?

(He knocks COD down.)

BRANDON: "Where be your gibes now? Your gambols? Your songs? Your
flashes of merriment?"

(Hits COD)

BRANDON: We always try to make you feel at home.

MAGGOT: *(To* BRANDON, *but also about her own past)* Get your fucking hands off—

COD: We have nothing to lose.

BRANDON: What did you say?

(Hits COD*)*

MAGGOT: No!

BRANDON: I didn't quite catch that?

MAGGOT: Don't.

BRANDON: You're mumbling. Girls shouldn't mumble. Nasty habit.

ROACH: Brandon!

BRANDON: Listen, young lady, I offered you that nice little office job, with a window to look out of. *(Starts to laugh)* But you couldn't handle it. *(Hits* COD *again)* No. I mean, this little bitch couldn't even read! Can you believe it? That's what he said. That's what he said to me: this little bitch can't even read!

*(*BRANDON *raises his arm to strike* COD *again, but* ROACH's *voice stops him.)*

ROACH: *(She plays the "boss" to get* BRANDON's *attention)* Can you believe it? This little bitch can't even read! How do you sign your name, then, baby, with what's left of your thumb? Can't you even defend yourself like a decent woman?

*(*BRANDON *is silent. He sinks to the floor.)*

ROACH: I didn't think so. You see, you're never gonna learn nothin', never gonna make nothin', never gonna be nothin'.

BRANDON: *(Whispers)* I can do it. I know I can do it.

ROACH: You're just a piece of gut got stuck to my shoe when I walked by.

*(*BRANDON *sits silent and numb. It is obvious that he is ill.)*

ROACH: I know, Brandon. I know it better than you. 'Cause that's what they've been saying to me all my life.

*(*TUCK *enters.)*

TUCK: What the hell's going on here? *(Sees* CODs *been hit)* Brandon's initiating the new crew again? Well, that's a "bingo". You're out, boy.

COD: No. Brandon was. He was showing me. How to—I slipped.

TUCK: Really? *(To* BRANDON*)* On your feet.

*(*BRANDON *doesn't respond.)*

ROACH: Get on the phone, Tuck, and call an ambulance. He needs medical attention.

*(*ROACH *helps* BRANDON *to his feet and leads him out.* TUCK *moves quick to call an ambulance.)*

COD: Local 226 is one of the last in the industry.

MAGGOT: Would you shut up already!? There's no difference anymore, union or not. Things just stay the same. Scrabblin' for something better is like scrabblin' for heaven. You only get there when you're dead.

COD: All we have to do is fold our arms, and the whole thing will stop.

MAGGOT: You really believe that?

COD: No. Not most of the time. But it's living under water like this.

MAGGOT: Yeah. And when you yell, it doesn't make a sound.

COD: Only bubbles.

MAGGOT: *(Shrugs)* What do you think about when you're working the meat? My hands do this thing called work, but I let my mind go somewhere else. Specially when the manager, that Baquin guy, comes to call. He likes to keep us neat, to tighten my apron when it gets loose, smooth the wrinkles down. *(Beat)* Does that excite you? Thinking about him touching me against my will?

COD: *(Puts his hand out into the air as though he were touching it)* Feel it? It's heatin' up in here.

MAGGOT: I don't mind the heat.

COD: Thats how it starts.

MAGGOT: It's the smell I can't get used to. *(Beat)* You're sweating.

COD: It's a hundred degrees in here. Who doesn't sweat?

MAGGOT: Maybe you're sick.

*(*MAGGOT *tries to touch* COD's *forehead to check his temperature, but* COD *jumps back, terrified at the thought of being touched.)*

COD: Don't. *(Beat)* Please.

MAGGOT: *(Amused)* Did you like it that time I kissed you?

COD: I wish I could say no.

MAGGOT: Take off your shirt. I want to see if you've got the kind of chest I like.

COD: What kind of chest is that?

MAGGOT: I'll know it when I see it.

COD: *(Turning away)* Things aren't always the way you see it.

(End Scene Ten)

Scene Eleven

(SAUSAGE MAN *appears, wandering in the empty packhouse as he speaks.* COD *sits nearby, huddled in a corner, dejected and alone. The* SAUSAGE MAN *knows* COD *is there, and his words are partly a performance for* COD.)

SAUSAGE MAN: What happened to the dream? Our dream? I made one sausage, then two, then three. I could live off of two and sell the third as surplus. The dream as simple math. Make more than you need. Sell the excess. With a little extra cash, hire some one to make the sausages for you, while you deal with the papers and the cash. What is unjust about having another human being work for you? I employed hundreds. I gave them free trimmings. But they bit the hand that fed them. Chomp. Chomp. They did not respect the math. The math of the dream. Myself, I am an innovator. I make something from the refuse in this world. And there will always be refuse in this world, so there will always be a place for me. It's just a matter of time, that's all.

(SAUSAGE MAN *nears* COD.)

SAUSAGE MAN: Tsk, tsk. I should have guessed. Daydreaming again. Wasting precious time.

COD: I hate it when you send me in as a scab instead of union; it takes twice as long to even get them to listen.

SAUSAGE MAN: A little extra challenge. You'll manage. You always do.

COD: Oh, leave me alone. Please.

SAUSAGE MAN: You're not ill, are you? (*Feels* COD's *forehead*) You shouldn't sit on the floor. It's damp.

(*The* SAUSAGE MAN *takes off his jacket and puts it around* COD's *shoulders*)

SAUSAGE MAN: You should take better care of yourself.

COD: A mollusc. In the ocean. A limpet. That's what I'd like to be.

SAUSAGE MAN: But they're so small. You might get eaten by a sea gull.

COD: Limpets live near reefs. They have this endless, tremendous ocean all around, but they stay their entire lives on one rock. And they never move from that rock. And if you try to pull a limpet off its rock, it hangs on. And the harder you pull, the more tightly it hangs on.

SAUSAGE MAN: How 'bout a walk? That'll cheer you up.

COD: I can't even imagine that kind of determination.

SAUSAGE MAN: Tsk, tsk. That's not very ambitious. A limpet? And what would you do then? Suck at a rock? For eternity?

COD: Yeah. And I'd be a part of it all. A part of the ocean. I'd watch the tide go in and out. I'd eat algae, digest sand, be witness to shipwrecks and sharks. The birth of an octopus. The death of a sea cow. My mate would be a starfish, and we'd grow old together. We'd even die. Imagine that? And millimeter by millimeter I'd travel that single rock. And after all those years—who knows?—maybe I'd even leave a scratch, some kind of mark on the stone to prove I was there.

(A noise somewhere that startles COD. *He clings to the* SAUSAGE MAN, *frightened.)*

What? What? Where are we?

SAUSAGE MAN: *(Holding him)* Shhh. We're still here. Shhh.

COD: *(Still clinging)* Where? Where?

SAUSAGE MAN: My child, why are you always lost? You've got to learn to locate yourself. Listen: This little piggy went to market. This little piggy stayed home. This little piggy—

COD: O K. Stop it. Stop it. I know where we are. But why a slaughterhouse? *(Looking* SAUSAGE MAN *over)* I preferred you as a Pullman, a Carnegie, or a Rockefeller, delving into mines, reeking of money, not meat.

SAUSAGE MAN: But you complained about the mines. Too much coal dust in the nose. And then you caught a cough, remember? That was a nasty cough you had.

COD: Yeah, and we were ready to blow that mountain wide open. The fuse was lit. But you yanked me out just before the explosion. Just in time.

SAUSAGE MAN: It might have been serious.

COD: Was it serious?

SAUSAGE MAN: Nasty. Sticky. There was a mess to clean up.

COD: What's the point if I never get to see things through? Damn you.

SAUSAGE MAN: That's it. Get angry! Tantrums make you hotter quicker.

*(*COD *turns away.)*

SAUSAGE MAN: Oh, come on now: kiss my forehead, child. *(Beat)* There's a life's work in this industry. Martyrs to be made. Reputations to be saved.

COD: I want something else. Anything. Forget the limpet then. Send me to an island. I'll rally the coconuts and crabs. I'll give you a good tussle. Only let me stay. In one place. Whatever the final outcome.

SAUSAGE MAN: I won't risk losing you.

COD: Then I'll refuse.

SAUSAGE MAN: It's your nature to resist. I can count on you. That's hard to come by in this late century. That sort of certainty. This city needs you.

COD: No. I need this city. Without you.

SAUSAGE MAN: *(Holds out his arm for the jacket)* The jacket, please. It's the only one I have.

(COD moves away.)

SAUSAGE MAN: Come now. I'm not a very convincing Mr Fisher without the threads, now am I? Do you want to be the death of me?

COD: *(Sniffing the jacket)* This jacket stinks.

SAUSAGE MAN: It's authentic. Mr Fisher died in it.

COD: Yeah? Well, alright then: meat this time it will be! *(He holds up the jacket.)* And how would you like your jacket sliced, sir?

SAUSAGE MAN: The sewing's a triple stitch. Take a look. Rather fine, isn't it?

COD: Fine did you say? One jacket, finely sliced, coming up. *(He takes a knife from his pocket.)* No fat on this one. *(He makes a neat, clean slice through the back of the jacket)*

SAUSAGE MAN: Now that's too bad.

(COD throws the jacket at the SAUSAGE MAN's feet. The SAUSAGE MAN puts it on. The rip down the back is visible.)

SAUSAGE MAN: Irreparable damage. No sense.

COD: I beg you.

SAUSAGE MAN: You're a fighter, Cod, not a beggar. Get out there and stir, spark, sputter. The laborer against my system! It's glorious. It's heroic. And we have all the time in the world. Do you know what that sounds like?

COD: I know what it tastes like. *(He spits on the floor.)* Like ashes on my tongue.

SAUSAGE MAN: Listen. *(He turns his grinder. We hear a strange, sad, and sensual music.)* That's the music of all the time in the world. Hear how it weeps, how it grieves and longs to be silent. But it can't. It must sing forever. Just like you. Dance to it, my child. Dance to your music.

(COD stands transfixed as the SAUSAGE MAN turns in a circle, like a figure in a music box, dancing to the music)

(End Scene Eleven)

Scene Twelve

(BAQUIN, TUCK, MAGGOT, and ROACH in BAQUIN's office)

BAQUIN: It's not the taste of our meat we're selling, but its appearance, its attitude. How the meat is colored, how it shines, how it carries itself with a straight spine, even if it's boneless. *(To* TUCK*)* Don't slouch. Bring me the soap and water. Good. A man won't get ahead if he slouches. But what's really getting the company image down is smudge, the smudginess of the workers. They aren't laundering their uniforms regularly.

TUCK: It's tough keeping a uniform clean down there, sir.

BAQUIN: One of your jobs is to make sure the work force looks decent. Would you say this work force looks decent? Look at the smudges, the wrinkles, the rips in the cloth.

TUCK: New uniforms were due six months ago.

BAQUIN: Nonsense. These uniforms are new. I ordered them myself. They simply haven't been cared for. We must cultivate a passion for cleanliness. The problem is that some of us simply lack passion, and passion is a clean impulse, not a dirty one. And where there is passion lacking, dirt will be lurking. *(Beat)* Take off the uniforms, please.

*(*MAGGOT *and* ROACH *look at each other in disbelief. They don't move.)*

BAQUIN: My dear ladies. Those uniforms are company property and the company wants to wash its property. Right now. *(Beat)* Take them off.

(The women turn away and begin to unbutton their uniforms. ROACH *turns to* TUCK *as she undresses. He turns to leave.* BAQUIN *silently stops* MAGGOT's *hand so that she stops undressing. Until she has removed her uniform,* ROACH *doesn't realize that she stands alone in her slip.)*

BAQUIN: Just a minute, Buck. I might need your help. Give them the soap and water.

*(*TUCK *places the bucket of soap and water between the two women.)*

ROACH: I can do this in the bathroom.

BAQUIN: This is private space here. Feel completely at home.

TUCK: *(Turning to leave again)* I need to check the pressure gauge on hog box number six, sir.

BAQUIN: That can wait. Now wash.

(The women don't wash.)

BAQUIN: *(Shouts)* Wash!

(The women take the sponges and begin to wash.)

BAQUIN: That's right. Get those smudges off. Scrub hard! Put that whiff of daintiness back in the cloth, restore that Odiferous Mundi. That's Latin for World Odor. The smell of worldliness and cleanliness. And we do need world odor. Order. Don't you agree, Chuck?

ROACH: *(Throws down her sponge)* We're finished.

BAQUIN: *(Looking* MAGGOT *over)* Yes. You are, Maggot. *(To* ROACH*)* But you can't be. *(He takes the sponge from* MAGGOT *and gently cleans a spot on her uniform.)* What do you think, Maggot? Is your friend clean?

*(*BAQUIN *continues sponging* MAGGOT, *slowly nearing, but not quite touching, her breasts.)*

TUCK: She's clean, sir.

BAQUIN: It's hard to tell. *(He sets a chair in the center.)* Roach, could you help us out? Please. Step up here so we can see things better?

(After some moments ROACH *steps up on the chair.)*

BAQUIN: Just as I suspected. There's dirt behind your knees.

TUCK: But, sir—

BAQUIN: Surely you can see it? Can't you, Maggot?

*(*MAGGOT *does not answer but looks away from* ROACH.*)*

BAQUIN: Exactly. Well put. Smudges are attracted to the backs of knees. Finish the job.

TUCK: Sir?

BAQUIN: Scrub behind her knees.

ROACH: Go on, Tuck. Follow your orders.

*(*TUCK *kneels before* ROACH *as she stands above him, though he doesn't wash her. She sings.)*

ROACH: Every day one more dolla in my hand
Slip through my fingers like a grain of sand

BAQUIN: *(To* TUCK*)* Let me see your nails.

TUCK & ROACH: *(Sing)* One day soon don'tcha know, I'll be free
Livin' in the sun so don't you worry 'bout me

BAQUIN: A supervisor must keep clean, short nails.

ROACH & TUCK: *(Sing)* O Lord, God hear me callin', take my hand

BAQUIN: Show me your hands.

*(*TUCK *puts his hands in his pockets.)*

ROACH & TUCK: *(Sing)* Won'tcha take me, take me to the promised land

BAQUIN: *(Shouts)* I said show me your hands!

ROACH & TUCK: O Lord, God hear me callin', take my hand won'tcha take me, take me to the promised land.

(After some moments of silence)

BAQUIN: Well, yes. Well. Tuck. I'm ravished. I'm going to catch a bite to eat. Please have their files ready. I'd like to look them over when I get back. *(Beat)* Would anyone like a cup of tea before they return to work?

(No response from the workers, so BAQUIN *shrugs and exits.)*

(End Scene Twelve)

Scene Thirteen

*(*COD *in the changing room.* MAGGOT *enters.* COD *has his shirt pulled up so we can see bandages around his lower back that he is just finishing retying.)*

COD: *(Looking over his shoulder)* Ladies, changing room is across the hall.

MAGGOT: What's the bandage for?

COD: *(Pulls down his shirt.)* Slipped on the kill floor. Got a steer horn in my ass. Cracked three ribs.

MAGGOT: Wait. Just wait. A minute.

(She approaches him. He does not turn around.)

MAGGOT: Can I touch your back?

COD: I'd rather you didn't.

MAGGOT: Oh.

COD: It's not that I don't like you.

MAGGOT: Sure.

COD: I wouldn't want you to make a mistake; I'm not the kind who sticks around.

MAGGOT: Save it.

COD: Look, you seem like. An interesting girl. Nice. If I could stay here a while, I would. But it's not up to me. I'm out of here, *(Snaps his fingers)* just like that, when he blows the whistle. Could be today. Could be tomorrow, and my time's up. And I don't leave a trace.

MAGGOT: I've heard *that* before.

*(*MAGGOT *is hardly listening to* COD. *She's moved closer to* COD *but hasn't touched him. Rather, she just stands there and feels the warmth coming from his back from a distance.)*

MAGGOT: I can feel the heat coming off your body like...You know, if I died, I think I'd like to lay my head down on something like you.

*(*COD *moves away.)*

COD: Who's thinking about dying?

MAGGOT: We don't have to think about it. We're already dead.

COD: Yeah. Most of the time. But then there's that minute or two, once or twice a year. Once or twice a decade, when you think, maybe this time something is gonna change.

MAGGOT: Nothing ever changes here. You just break down after so many years, and they sweep you out back with the rest of the scraps.

COD: Whatever happened to that animal called hope?

MAGGOT: First it got stunned, then it got slaughtered. Seems like for years I just wake and work and shit and sleep. It's a good life. Nothing to disappoint me. *(Beat)* You know, when I was a kid there were only two things I wanted in the world. A V-8 pickup and a boyfriend who'd let me drive. You wouldn't think that was a lot to ask for in life, would you?

(End Scene Thirteen)

Scene Fourteen

(ROACH and MAGGOT at the end of the day in the changing room. ROACH has her rod and lure box with her. She opens the lure box and sorts them, getting ready for the weekend.)

MAGGOT: The truth is, my uniform was cleaner than yours.

ROACH: Get your narrow white ass out of my face—

MAGGOT: Yeah? You look like garbage. You never take your uniform home and bleach the stains out, like I do.

ROACH: You know what I was thinking when I stood on that chair? No. You don't know. You have no idea.

MAGGOT: What was I supposed to do?

ROACH: Not one word. Didn't call my name. Didn't say, I'm here by your side. Nothing.

MAGGOT: You didn't do nothing either. Should I've let him get me like that too? Then we could've both played the dog. Oh yeah. That woulda been "right on, sister". *(Beat)* I couldn't have been that kind of friend to anyone.

ROACH: *(Examines lures while ignoring MAGGOT)* Ah, the rapalla. Looks like a knife in the water.

MAGGOT: I thought I could, but I guess I can't.

ROACH: Nickname: "Stab in the back." *(Holds up another lure)* Double-headed jig. I call her "Old two-face-strikes-again."

MAGGOT: I'm not making my bills.

ROACH: *(Holds up another lure)* Big eyes: the Zephyr Puppy. Commonly know as: the traitor.

MAGGOT: I don't want to sell the truck. Could sell the tires.

ROACH: Oh, she plays it coy.

MAGGOT: God damn it, I'm tired.

ROACH: But she's got nine silver hooks, nine pretty lies just waiting for you.

MAGGOT: You don't know what that's like. I can't even get myself off any more 'cause my hands start to shake so bad when I go into repetitive motion.

ROACH: Whoever named it carpal tunnel never had it. Sounds like a fish.

MAGGOT: I was on probation last summer, remember? You piss too often, you chew your lunch too slow, your sausages aren't bent the right way. Well, I got called down to the office. My scales were off about half a point. Manager said he'd have to let me go. I said I needed the job. He said how bad. I said bad. He said show me. *(Beat)* I showed him. *(Beat)* Across his desk between two fern plants.

(They are silent some moments.)

ROACH: I hate ferns.

MAGGOT: Whatever it was you wanted me to do that day, I just couldn't do it. I guess I'm not who I thought I was.

ROACH: That makes two of us.

MAGGOT: You know, when I was a kid I couldn't sleep at night, thinking about dying. Now I think about dying the way I fix a bowl of cereal in the morning; I could take it or leave it.

ROACH: You remember Mr Morton? Our second-grade teacher? You used to get jealous, 'cause he would take me fishing and he wouldn't ever take you.

MAGGOT: I remember: Teacher's pet.

ROACH: Yeah, well, he liked fishing the way I liked it and sometimes after school he'd take me down to the stream. He was the first white man who ever treated me like a child likes to be treated. Like I had something special about me that only he could see. *(Beat)* When Mr Morton cast a good line, his ears would go red. Red as a worm.

MAGGOT: *(Sings)* Oh, my love is like a red, red, worm.

ROACH: They say a worm has seven hearts and that if you break it up in the right places, two or three of the pieces will live. Problem was, I never knew where the hearts were or where to put the hook in. That's why I mostly use artificials now. *(She casts her rod as if out into the audience and reels it back in.)* Twelve-pound line. Eight-pound line. I was using a six-pound line that day and I landed a four-pound small-mouth bass. You remember the picture? That fish was longer than my arm! Almost snapped my line. Mr Morton and

I skinned it right there and cooked it over the fire. I can tell you I was proud that day. And Mr Morton was proud of me too. He kissed me on the mouth four times, one kiss for each pound of that bass. Have you ever made your teacher that proud of you? I liked him better than my own father because he took me fishing and my own father never had time because he was always at the packhouse splittin' hogs. *(Beat)* Four times. On the mouth. He said he wanted to know what my kind... tasted like. *(Beat)* That's how proud he was. That's how. Yes. And I closed my eyes, because if a worm has seven hearts it could have eight and I wanted him to know I could take it. And I took it. Right there in the grass beside the stream. *(Beat)* But once it's cut you never can tell just which parts of the worm have been killed and which parts will crawl away and start over because all of the parts are moving. All of the parts are trying to live. Funny. How you can look at a body and see nothing but the whole of it. But I know. I know which parts went on and lived and which parts gave up and died.

(MAGGOT *just watches her in silence*)

ROACH: Yeah. I *know* what it's like, girl. I just don't let it lead me. *(Beat)* Damn it. I oughta punch you in the mouth *(Beat)* but it's the weekend and you and me are going fishing!

(End Scene Fourteen)

Scene Fifteen

(COD *and the* SAUSAGE MAN *in the empty packhouse, at night*)

COD: Let go of me.

SAUSAGE MAN: You're becoming tiresome, Cod.

COD: I need to stay here.

SAUSAGE MAN: Tiresome is not fun. You're meant to be my rival, not a driveling pup!

COD: Just a little bit longer.

SAUSAGE MAN: Well, well. I think you've finally fallen in love. How sweet. How infantile. Tell me, has she seen you out of this garb?

COD: This garb? You think I'd have had a chance in hell of catching their attention—of catching anyone's attention in the last fifteen decades—if I hadn't worn this garb?

SAUSAGE MAN: Come now. You've always enjoyed a nice cut pair of trousers.

COD: Listen to me: She could keep me here.

SAUSAGE MAN: Ah, yes. The strength of a woman's love to break an old promise? I like it. But what are you waiting for? Why don't you sweep her up in your arms?

COD: Because if I touch what I desire—I'll destroy it—Just one touch and...toast.

SAUSAGE MAN: That's right. You can't touch her. Not like *that*. And don't you forget it.

COD: I hate these hands.

SAUSAGE MAN: You can't change the past, Cod. It's like you, condemned to repeat itself.

COD: Yeah. And I'm always at your mercy, because once upon a time someone somewhere agreed that yours was the only game. But what if there were another way?

SAUSAGE MAN: Imagine that! How exciting.

COD: What if, over time, all this friction, all this fire, began to burn a hole in your playground?

SAUSAGE MAN: That's my Cod! Keep tossing those dice.

COD: Then we'd just walk through that hole to the other side. And from the stink and wreckage of your death, we'd build something new.

SAUSAGE MAN: Give it your best shot!

COD: But I never get to stay around long enough to see what's left, do I?

SAUSAGE MAN: Don't be sour. You're a spark for eternity. What else could you ask for?

COD: What else? What else? *(Beat)* Just for one single moment to be without heat. To shiver. Watch my fingers turn blue. To be *(Beat)* cold. Yeah. That's what I'd like. To be cold like...snow.

SAUSAGE MAN: *(Grinds his sausage machine. As he does so, it begins to snow inside the packhouse:)* To be cold like snow.

(COD looks up in amazement and lifts his arms to catch the snow like a child might.)

SAUSAGE MAN: In your dreams, my friend. Only in your dreams.

(End Scene Fifteen)

END ACT ONE

ACT TWO

Scene One

(COD, MAGGOT, *and* ROACH *are listening to* BAQUIN, *who stands in the center of the work room,* TUCK *at his side. The workers all have their arms raised.*)

BAQUIN: Let's try it again. Ready? And a one, two, three, go!

(BAQUIN *and* TUCK *do jumping jacks. The workers stand with arms raised but they don't jump. After eight jumps or so,* TUCK *stops. Then* BAQUIN *stops.*)

BAQUIN: Not just your arms, but your feet too. You've got to moooooove...
You've got to mooooove. (*He clears his throat.*) Jump up and down.
Like I do. You've got to learn to take care of your bodies. Your body
is a temple. It belongs to God. Your body is God's property. Respect God's
property. Respect God's temple with its rooms, oh, gorgeous rooms—
So jump! Leap! Exercise your gifts. Raise your bodies to the cause, make
yourselves stars of motivation, coordination, innovation! (*Beat*) Now.
Let's try it again. And this time make an effort. And a one, two, three, go!

(*Everyone does jumping jacks in unison for some moments. One by one they stop—first* ROACH, *then* MAGGOT, *then* COD, *then* TUCK, *then* BAQUIN.)

BAQUIN: Now take a deep breath. In, and out. In, and out. Well, I feel
refreshed. How about the rest of you?

(*No response. The workers stare at him.* BAQUIN *exits, then* COD *and* MAGGOT.
TUCK *and* ROACH *are alone.*)

TUCK: It's Miss Roach, isn't it?

ROACH: Miss Lyles. Roach is my first name.

TUCK: You taught the recorder lessons after work for employees?

ROACH: That was Maggot.

TUCK: Could I ask where you got your name?

ROACH: Little girl gave it to me when I was seven. I collected bugs.
The day I met her I only had a roach in my bug box. So she called
me Roach. That was Maggot. Maggot calls me Roach.

TUCK: That's a name that won't get you very far.

ROACH: It's not my name that's holding me back.

TUCK: And Maggot?

ROACH: When I met her she looked whiter than any white kid I'd ever met. She reminded me of a maggot. The whiteness of maggots.

TUCK: Yes. I can see how it came to you. White friend. That sounds like a contradiction.

ROACH: Sometimes it is.

TUCK: Well, Roach. What do you know about snails?

(ROACH *just looks at him.*)

TUCK: *Partula affinis.* It is the last snail of its kind. This packing company is going to start a committee to raise funds for a search in the South Pacific. For a mate. I'd like you to head the steering committee. We'll call it the Salvation Nature Alliance Involving Laborers. S-N-A-I-L. Snail. *(Beat)* The board's hot on the idea. They've asked me to sell it.

ROACH: We get a new contract signed, and I'll get you members for Snail.

TUCK: You do trimming, right? Number three pay bracket? How would you like ham pumper or pickle maker?

ROACH: Can we speak off the record?

TUCK: Of course.

ROACH: Last year the Company tried to sell us piano lessons after work. The year before, it was ice skating for management and employees on Sunday afternoons. Free of charge. Well, let me tell you something: we're at war here. And we will not shake your hand and we will not skate with you and we will not sing Christmas carols with you for the holidays. We have nothing in common, Tuck. Nothing. And it's a sorry thing when people like you don't even have to be forced to the hook. No. Worms like you jump on the hook, take the spear right in their gut and then wriggle and say they like it. You may be a supervisor, Tuck, but you're still a nigger, and when he's through with you, you'll go out with the rest of the garbage. *(Beat)* I'll see you there.

TUCK: How about a smoker? Top pay bracket. Or a cooker? You can have your pick. *(Beat)* It's not a color thing anymore, Miss Roach. It's a money thing, a class thing.

ROACH: Yeah. It's a money thing alright, and I haven't got any. But I have got a class and you, my brother, are not in it. But you might be again one day. Because the color thing never quite rubs off. You know it and I know it.

(*He touches her hair, briefly.*)

TUCK: I'm sorry about the uniforms. It wasn't my idea.

ROACH: When I see you back on the kill floor, then we'll do some talking.

TUCK: Frankly, I don't like snails myself.

ROACH: Don't get in our way.

(End Scene One)

Scene Two

(MAGGOT, ROACH, and COD are working in the refrigeration unit among large, hanging carcasses, stamping the meat. They all sing together. The song is less celebration than a song of exhaustion and despair.)

MAGGOT, ROACH, & COD:
We stick and slit and shackle and head
We snap and trim and pull and scald
We scale and stun and scrape the meat
We pack it all for you to eat.

If there's a hell it's as hot as this
Standing all day in the blood and piss
We work in the war zone and the wages we pull
Aren't enough to keep a dog's tit full.

(BRANDON enters, moving slowly, like someone who has recently been ill. He steels his knife, very slowly.)

BRANDON: *(To COD)* Let me see your knife.

(COD hands the knife over. BRANDON examines the blade.)

BRANDON: You sharpen this?

COD: Yes, I did.

BRANDON: Manually, I see.

COD: Yes.

BRANDON: Good for you. But you've folded the edge over. Cutting with a knife like this you'll pull your back out. Look. It won't cut.

(BRANDON reaches for COD's hand, but COD pulls back. BRANDON rolls up his own sleeve and drags the blade down his arm. It doesn't cut him.)

BRANDON: See what I mean? *(Holds the knife up between them)* The edge of a knife if like a thin piece of hair. If you angle that steel wrong, you're going to fold the edge over.

COD: I'll work at it.

(COD returns to work.)

BRANDON: So the company won't talk?

MAGGOT: Sent them three proposals. They said no.

ROACH: And no and no.

COD: They'll bring in replacements if we strike again.

BRANDON: So it's "we" now, is it? *(Beat)* I heard about the new proposal while I was...out. So we've offered to cut knife time in exchange for seniority rights?

ROACH: We had to give them something. We're fucking tired. Half voted to throw in the towel. Next time we vote, it'll be over. And so will we.

BRANDON: We're not going to eat their contract. Ever. Isn't that what we said? *(Speaks even slower)* See how a few...few...thousand wa...wa...watts to the brain can make a fell...fellow...rea...rea...rea...sonable? *(Suddenly he jumps and does a perfect cartwheel and ends up face to face with* ROACH, *speaking fast, in rhythm.)* So. Have you made a decision
'tween makin' the dip
to sip the straw
or having a dip on a cone
while I sup with my cup
and smile my way up?

MAGGOT: We didn't miss you, Brandon.

(End Scene Two)

Scene Three

(We are back in the workroom with COD *and the* TEXTILE WORKER. *It is the same dream/scene as the prelude. The* TEXTILE WORKER *is the central focus, but we also see* MAGGOT, ROACH, *and* BRANDON *working slowly, in silence. They are not aware of the scene going on around them, though they will chant with the woman.)*

TEXTILE WORKER: *(Chants)* Pull the cloth, punch it down, cut three out, and trace.

COD: Hey! I'm talking to you!

TEXTILE WORKER: Hurry, hurry, don't go slow, keep your cheer and grace.

COD: I know you can hear me.

TEXTILE WORKER: Pull the cloth, punch it down—

COD: Look at me!

TEXTILE WORKER: *(Turns to look at him but looks in another direction, away from* COD *as though she sees* COD *elsewhere)* I am looking at you. I'm always looking at you.

(Smoke begins to trickle in from a crack in the floor.)

COD: No. No.

TEXTILE WORKER: Yes. Look at your hands. They're beautiful. *(She holds up her own hands.)* Like mine once were.

COD: Can't you see what's happening?!

TEXTILE WORKER: Your hands are like two flames.

COD: Do something!

TEXTILE WORKER: All the water in the world can't put their fire out.

(COD drops to his knees and tries to cover the smoke with his hands to keep it from coming in.)

COD: There's no fire. There's no smoke. Not here. So pull the cloth, punch it down.

(The SAUSAGE MAN enters with his sausage machine.)

ALL THE WORKERS: "Cut three out and trace."

SAUSAGE MAN: The doors have been locked.

TEXTILE WORKER: "Hurry, hurry, don't be slow—"

SAUSAGE MAN: From the outside.

ALL THE WORKERS: "—keep your cheer and grace."

SAUSAGE MAN: To keep track of employees. The fire trucks are on their way. The fireman will say his ladders could only reach the seventh floor. Is this the eighth?

COD: Let us out. Open the fucking doors!

SAUSAGE MAN: I don't have the key. I lost it years ago. *(Beat)* It's already happened. You can't change it. Why upset yourself?

COD: *(Turns to the other workers)* Help me with the doors. We'll break them down.

(The workers go on working. They can't hear him.)

COD: You stupid bastards.

SAUSAGE MAN: They can't hear you.

TEXTILE WORKER: My hands sweep the cloth like water—

COD: *(To the workers)* Do you want to die?

TEXTILE WORKER: *(Continuing)* —over the keys of a piano.

COD: Are you just going to stand there and burn?

(SAUSAGE MAN cranks his grinder, and the fire increases. The workers go on working.)

SAUSAGE MAN: They won't ever be able to hear you. Because you're always somewhere else, my child.

COD: *(Sinking down to the floor as in the first fire scene. At the moment he shouts the sound of the fire increases to drown out his voice.)* Isn't anybody out there!

(End Scene Three)

Scene Four

*(*TUCK *alone on stage in* BAQUIN's *office. The chair* ROACH *stood on still stands center stage. He sees it. He circles it. He slowly gets undressed, then stands on the chair, as* ROACH *did earlier. He stands still some moments, as though in another place and/or time. In his mind, he hears* ROACH *singing a line of the song she sang when she stood on the chair in* BAQUIN's *office. Then* TUCK *gets off the chair. He picks up his clothes. As he casually exits, he reaches out and tips the chair over with one finger.)*

(End Scene Four)

Scene Five

*(*COD *and* BRANDON *in the cafeteria.* BRANDON *is seated, engrossed in eating.)*

COD: It's a scandal.

BRANDON: Make yourself at home. Food's not that bad.

COD: O K. Then as food it shall be.

BRANDON: It is food.

COD: Not always it isn't.

BRANDON: What is the "it" we're talking about here?

COD: It's no longer an "it", it's an "isn't".

BRANDON: You're ruining my lunch with your gibberish. Can't a man have—

COD: A man should have.

BRANDON: A peaceful...intermission? *(Returns to his food)*

COD: *(Picking items off* BRANDON's *plate)* Not this canned pea, not this frozen carrot, in fact, not even this...

BRANDON: Lumpagravy.

COD: Right. Not one piece of anything comes into being without us.

BRANDON: So, what's new?

COD: Not even this tray. *(He takes* BRANDON's *tray.)*

BRANDON: Wait a minute.

COD: What you see here is dead.

BRANDON: It's a pork chop.

COD: Labor. Dead labor, of past and present.

BRANDON: Get out of my lunch.

(COD *lifts the tray and balances it between them, then swiftly slams it onto the table, face down.* BRANDON *watches, stunned.*)

COD: Without the tray, the mashed potatoes slide into the cheesecake, the milk swamps the peas. This is the situation we're in today. Without the tray, and the tray being the union here, we're without a world that gives us definition and power. We're no longer a community of carrots and peas and mashed potatoes— (COD *grabs a handful of the squashed food up in his hand.*) —but a handful of slops. And they'll use us to feed the hogs.

BRANDON: *(Picks the pork chop out of the mess) Voilà!* The pork chop's the enemy, right?

COD: You got it.

BRANDON: What's the Big Bad Boss doing down here in the mess with the rest of us?

COD: No, no. The pork chop is the enemy in disguise. The pork chop's no better off than the peas. The pork chop's—

BRANDON: The scab.

COD: Bingo.

(BRANDON *eats the pork chop.*)

COD: What you see here is deregulation so that workers have no way of protecting their rights. When we make a stink 'cause we're offered part-time jobs with twelve-hour shifts, big business just ups and moves over the border or across the sea. It's the sort of unsavory wage situation you see here when your milk and gravy meet the cheesecake and it begins to dissolve.

BRANDON: If we were having Jello, it wouldn't have made a whole lot of difference.

COD: There's always room for Jello, because we're one of the only industrialized nations where illegal firings and the hiring of scabs are common practice.

BRANDON: Those fucking pork chops.

(COD *hands* BRANDON *a fork and takes a spoon.*)

COD: We're back to the Depression. Eat. No. Back to the Victorian age. *(He eats from the table.)* Robber Barons are again free to trade—eat!—over our dying bodies. Everything and nothing has changed.

(BRANDON, *to his own surprise, eats from the mess as well.*)

COD: But guess what? (*Pounds on the food with fork*) No matter how many times they pull the tray out from under us, smash, mash, and pulverize our communities— (*Takes another bite*) We're still here.

BRANDON: And we're still eating.

COD: Right. (*Beat*) You have the cheesecake. (*Looking the food over*) If you can find it.

(*End Scene Five*)

Scene Six

(COD *and* MAGGOT *are on break.* COD *is checking over his belt tools.*)

MAGGOT: A 1965 baby-blue F-100 Ford, long bed, with a V-8 so hot I can blow the pants off the highway in third gear.

COD: Must be some truck.

MAGGOT: Yeah. Only it's sitting in my yard right now with a main seal leak and bad mounts. I'm doing the bus these days. You a compact man?

COD: I know a good truck.

MAGGOT: Well, you don't know my truck. I'm the only one who can drive it, 'cause it's three-on-a tree and it sticks in second.

COD: Fords are temperamental.

MAGGOT: Yeah. The engine sweats, foams just a little at the edges. The trick isn't in your hand, really; it's in your groin. You got to rock your hips at just the right rhythm to lubricate the hitch on that second gear.

COD: I could drive a truck like that.

MAGGOT: Ever changed gears with your mouth? Not too tight and when the pressure's right and just about to blow, you open it up, wide, and shoot across that highway with the windshield shattering over your head like snow and the sun pouring down your throat like water. And there's no turning back.

COD: Ford, huh? A person could go to hell for driving a Ford. They'll put a stick shift up your ass, and the Devil will cruise you all over his Island singing, "Ford-gives-you-better-ideas". All through eternity.

MAGGOT: Should have figured you were Chevy.

COD: A '58, V-8, short bed with chrome hubs, A M radio, four on the floor and no hitch. But not everyone can drive a Chevy. You got to have the proper wrist action or you'll burn the gears. And if your hands are dry— (*Spits in palm*) —you won't get the grip you need. (*Takes out a screwdriver or other sharp work tool)* You drive a Ford soft, but a Chevy's got to be treated rough. It's what a Chevy likes, 'cause it's an immoral engine and it can take it. Slap it some gas in first and, when you have the speed up and the friction between the rubber and the road is sending sparks down your spine—

(COD *sticks the screw driver into the ground or box between* MAGGOT's *legs. This should be done suddenly and would frighten anyone but* MAGGOT. COD *takes hold of the screw driver as though it were a stick shift between* MAGGOT's *legs.)*

COD: —then fast into second, straight on and hard. *(Moves stick into second)* Now third's a risk. Third is going down on the engine. But you got to keep up the speed. And speed isn't a motion, it's a texture. And it's not dry. No. Speed is wet. Speed is an ocean, and third's a deep gear, a diver's gear, only for the brave at heart gear, and I open up the vents 'cause my cylinders need some air, and then down, down— *(Moves stick into third, closer to* MAGGOT's *crotch)* —and lock into third.

(Some moments of silence)

MAGGOT: And what about the last one: fourth gear?

(COD *unsticks the screw driver and turns away to finish checking his tool belt.)*

MAGGOT: Hey! What about fourth gear?

COD: I never tell a girl how to get into fourth gear. She's got to find that out herself. I will tell you it's not about breaking the sound barrier. It's about breaking light, just like breaking ice under your wheels.

MAGGOT: Never met anyone like you.

COD: I'm not surprised. Want to see a trick? *(He touches the floor with his hand, and, where he touches it he leaves an imprint of his hand that starts to smoke.)*

MAGGOT: Aren't we the Boy Scout!

COD: With some women it works.

MAGGOT: Son of a bitch.

COD: Don't think so; Never knew my mother. She died in the fire...in Peoria, Illinois. A coat factory. No. That's not it. It was the.... No... Yes...the... Triangle Shirtwaist Company...in New York City, some time ago. Turn of the century.

MAGGOT: Just when were you born?

COD: The fire started in a rag bin on the seventh floor, swept through the eighth, ninth, and tenth floors. Mostly young women. My mother jumped. A lot of them did. They went in pairs. Holding hands. Nothing below them but concrete. My mother landed on top of some others. She wasn't crushed up like the rest of them. I was inside her. She was dead, but I wasn't. When the doctors found out I was in there, they ventilated her for five months. It was an experiment. They'd already filled out her death certificate. Then they cut her open and took me out.

MAGGOT: I heard about that fire.

COD: Yeah. I was born from a dead woman.

MAGGOT: That fire happened over eighty years ago.

COD: *(Wryly)* It's a hell of a way to come in to the world.

(End Scene Six)

Scene Seven

(BRANDON sneaks into the women's changing room. He's not sure what he's looking for. He sees a woman's work dress. He smells and touches it in much the same way as he did in Act One, Scene Ten.)

BRANDON: "I have lain in prison...Out of my nature has come wild despair—

(He takes the dress in his arms. ROACH enters, watches unobserved for some moments.)

BRANDON: —an abandonment to grief that was piteous even to look at." *(Beat)* No. Not on your knees. *(He tries again.)* My darling, my dreams are dark, dark, dark. *(Beat)* Damn. Don't bring up color. *(He tries again.)* When I am with you, I feel the...the shadows of our desire floating and...light, no...floating and...luminous above us, delirious with..with...intercourse. Intercourse? Shit. *(Beat)* Can I hold your hand?

ROACH: *(Appears)* Now I like this show better than the last one, cherub. But you could use some lessons. *(Beat)* Put the dress on.

(They watch each other some moments.)

ROACH: I mean it.

(BRANDON glances quickly over his shoulder to make sure they're alone.)

BRANDON: Please, sir. Avert your eyes. *(He takes off his clothes, turning away to do so.)* No peeking!

(ROACH watches him undress and put the dress on as he speaks the following.)

BRANDON: Oh, I'm just a girl, a waif like a wafer you could snap in two, just a gosling in distress, an egret with no inlet to satisfy my pitiable appetites.

ROACH: Shush up, baby doll. Or I'll tear your fucking heart out with my teeth.

BRANDON: Oh, no, no, no. *(Beat)* Oh, yes, yes, yes.

(ROACH is silent.)

BRANDON: Well, go on, you brute. Tear me into tiny, little pieces.

ROACH: I forget the script.

BRANDON: Now you force me.

ROACH: I force you.

BRANDON: Yeah. *(Beat)* Please, please, pretty please.

ROACH: *(Approaches* BRANDON *and takes hold of the collar of the dress)* Isn't this the part where I....

BRANDON: Exactly.

ROACH: And I do it all the way down....

BRANDON: You got it.

ROACH: I won't be able to wear it again if I do that.

BRANDON: Don't worry, darling, I've got one at home I can lend you...

ROACH: Shut up.

(ROACH *rips the dress open so that* BRANDON's *chest is exposed. This should be done how we've seen it in countless melodramatic films.)*

ROACH: I could get into this style.

BRANDON: And now you...go on...now you...

ROACH: Chew your mouth up, right?

BRANDON: And the eternal flames of hell engulf us.

ROACH: I don't think so.

BRANDON: Trespass matures the soul.

ROACH: It wouldn't be a game out there, Brandon.

BRANDON: This is the nineties.

ROACH: A Puerto Rican friend of mine had some teeth kicked out for dating a white girl.

BRANDON: My friends won't mind; I don't have any.

ROACH: What's the deal? Does it make you feel bad 'cause I'm black?

BRANDON: You want me.

ROACH: You're a boy, Brandon.

BRANDON: You want me and you hate me for it.

ROACH: This is a kid's game. I'm not playing.

BRANDON: You're a coward.

ROACH: I just like things simple.

BRANDON: Look. These are the facts. I like your mouth. It's the only place on earth I ever felt like laying a foundation to make a home.

ROACH: This wouldn't be simple.

BRANDON: I have this dream sometimes. And in the dream the scars on my mouth are gone, and my mouth is...like it's...scorched, seared, and then you kiss me and your kiss is so cold. (*He gently runs a finger over her lips.*) Like an apple in the snow.

(ROACH *removes* BRANDON's *hand.*)

BRANDON: When I wake up from that kiss, my pillow is always wet and I'm crying like a baby.

ROACH: A kiss is a dangerous thing.

BRANDON: It's a dangerous thing to live without it. (*Beat*) Are you afraid of me?

ROACH: (*Laughs*) I'm afraid of me.

BRANDON: I won't give it up.

ROACH: No. I don't think you will. Alright. (*She takes one of* BRANDON's *knives.*) I'll give you a kiss. If.

BRANDON: If?

ROACH: If you can take this knife from me. (*Beat*) But if either one of us bleeds, if either one of us gets so much as a paper cut, it's over. And we'll never talk about us again. Agreed? (*Beat*) Agreed?

BRANDON: Yeah. Completely.

(ROACH *puts the blade between her teeth. Slowly and carefully she passes the knife from her mouth to* BRANDON's *mouth. In doing this, they are also in a kiss. During this transfer,* BRANDON *is pushed to his knees. He now holds the knife between his teeth as he kneels*)

ROACH: That's where I like my Tarzan. On his knees.

(*End Scene Seven*)

Scene Eight

(MAGGOT *and* ROACH *on break.* MAGGOT *is smoking.* ROACH *drinks a glass of water. They hardly hear what the other is saying.*)

MAGGOT: I've been thinking about trading the Ford.

ROACH: He's a kid. But he's a smart kid.

MAGGOT: You ever had a Chevy?

ROACH: He's not really a kid, I mean, he's twenty-two. That's about....
(She counts on her fingers.)

MAGGOT: A Chevy can take a lot of rust.

ROACH: Not so bad.

MAGGOT: And the front end won't go out at a hundred thousand.

ROACH: But he's awfully white. Don't you think he's awfully white?

MAGGOT: He's Irish. They don't get much sun.

ROACH: A bit young and a bit white.

MAGGOT: How much older are you, about a decade?

ROACH: Thanks.

MAGGOT: I love you, you know.

ROACH: What's out there will keep coming between you and me. If you ever forget it, we're finished. When it comes down to it, they're going to try and break one of us, and, more likely than not, it's going to be me. And you're going to stand by and watch.

MAGGOT: I couldn't get a job anywhere else.

ROACH: You couldn't get a friend like me anywhere else.

MAGGOT: That's for sure.

ROACH: So has he got a spotty ass?

MAGGOT: I haven't got that close yet. *(Beat)* I've had some crushes, you know, pretty serious before. But I never felt like the ones I knew could reach down inside me, grab a hold of my tail bone and turn me inside out, like a shirt.

ROACH: I know what you mean.

MAGGOT: And Cod's got this smell.... Ahhh... A smell like...like something that's just about to burn.

ROACH: I kissed Brandon the other day.

MAGGOT: No!

ROACH: It was...interesting.

MAGGOT: Interesting? What's he taste like?

ROACH: Like nothing. *(Beat)* Nice.

MAGGOT: This one's over my head.

(ROACH turns around.)

ROACH: Yeah. It is. *(Beat)* Close your eyes.

(MAGGOT does. ROACH tilts MAGGOT's face up.)

ROACH: Brandon tastes...

(She pours the water slowly and gently onto MAGGOT's *face.)*

ROACH: Like this. Like water. Like drinking one, two, three glasses of water.

(End Scene Eight)

Scene Nine

(ROACH *and* MAGGOT *are still standing together in the shadows. The* SAUSAGE MAN *appears. No one sees him but* COD.)

SAUSAGE MAN: It's time for you to go.

COD: Not yet.

SAUSAGE MAN: I can feel the heat coming off your body a hundred years from now. Why don't we go there?

COD: I'm not leaving this time.

SAUSAGE MAN: You're trying my patience.

COD: Hey, all of you. Look at this son of a bitch!

(Neither ROACH *nor* MAGGOT *hear* COD.)

SAUSAGE MAN: I've let you stay far too long already.

COD: Check this joker out!

SAUSAGE MAN: Listen, I'm getting tired of playing rivals.

COD: Go back to the hell you crawled out of.

SAUSAGE MAN: I want you to come work for me. On my side this time. We'd make a good team. You're sensitive. You listen to the meat. You'd know how to coax it into my grinder without a struggle. Without a strike. We could start anew.

COD: This time it's going to be different.

(ROACH exits. MAGGOT *remains on stage, finishing her cigarette.* COD *turns away from* SAUSAGE MAN.)

COD: I can't touch her. I can't. You know that. I can't touch anyone like that. I'd burn them to a cinder. Turn their heart to a chunk of coal. But in my head. No. That you can't stop. In my head I touch her over and over. Again and again.

(COD approaches MAGGOT *closely, but* MAGGOT *is unaware of* COD.)

COD: And her skin is cold and sweet. Ice forms at the corners of her mouth. Just before we kiss. And across the world it's winter. In the fields. Inside the houses. Even under our tongues. Winter.

(MAGGOT *exits.*)

COD: But, even in my own head, I can't make her touch me. Because I don't know what it's like to be touched. What? What? Does it cut or maul? Scratch or tear? Tell me. Is it pain? You don't know. But it must be pain, because my heart is a cheap toy and it breaks inside my chest each time I try to imagine: What would it feel like to have her hand on my breast, her fingers along my spine. Her hard mouth against my hip. And what would it be like to stop moving at that touch? To stand still and listen? Just listen. To the pulse in her wrist. No rage, no hurry, no you and me, no struggle. Just her blood, to and fro, in her wrist, against my ear. *(Beat)* I am alone. I have never been anything but alone. Let her touch me. And I'll know where I am.

SAUSAGE MAN: What a sermonizer the decades have made you. You'd've made your mother proud. But reality won't be changed, Cod.

COD: It's nothing more than a bucket of clay, and this time we're going to shape it.

SAUSAGE MAN: It might go bad if you push me. Things aren't ripe yet.

COD: Yeah, well sometimes history's just not ready for you and so you give it a shove.

SAUSAGE MAN: Snap of my fingers and you're toad's dust.

COD: But then there's no conflict. And if there's no conflict, then I won't exist. And neither will you. *(Beat)* You can send me anywhere, but you can't make me fight you; I quit.

SAUSAGE MAN: Damn you. Damn you! *(Beat)* Alright. If you won't play, then you'll have to pay. But how much?

(He *gestures to the shadows, where in the darkness we see the shadow of the* TEXTILE WORKER *working. She shines with a strange light.*)

SAUSAGE MAN: How much will you pay? *(Beat)* Listen. "Pull the cloth, punch it down, cut three out, and trace." Can you hear her? She's talking. Oh, yes, and laughing. Because it's Friday and it's almost time to quit work.

(COD *puts his hands over his ears so he won't hear* SAUSAGE MAN, *who seems to be physically hurting him by recounting the story.*)

SAUSAGE MAN: And she feels you kick inside her, and she whispers something to you, and she is happy because she's managed to borrow a crib from a friend and because the woman sitting across from her is telling a joke about Jack be nimble, Jack be quick, Jack tripped over the candlestick. Stupid, stupid Jack. Now flames are coming up through the floor boards at her feet. Can you hear her, Cod? She's not laughing anymore. No. She's making another sound now. Listen.

(We hear the sound of pressure being released, the sound of something bursting forth from its restraints. Then we hear a terrible scream of pain from offstage. At the same moment of the scream, COD and the TEXTILE WORKER shout.)

COD & TEXTILE WORKER: No!

(End Scene Nine)

Scene Ten

(BRANDON is lying on the floor. ROACH and COD are beside him. MAGGOT paces.)

MAGGOT: Ten minutes. They said ten minutes.

ROACH: Where's the fucking first aid! He's not breathing.

COD: *(To MAGGOT)* Call the fire department.

ROACH: He's not breathing!

COD: Tell them we got an ammonia line break at hog-box number six.

(MAGGOT exits.)

ROACH: That's it, Brandon. Breathe. Breathe. Slow. Breathe slow.

(BRANDON's lungs make a terrible sounds as he tries to breathe.)

COD: *(Shouts to off-stage)* Maggot? Get him some water. Maggot?

(BRANDON tries to speak but can't.)

ROACH: Shhhh. Just breathe.

BRANDON: *(He begins to struggle.)* Fuck.

COD: *(Shouts)* Maggot?! *(To ROACH)* Keep his head back.

(COD takes out a knife.)

ROACH: What the hell are you doing?

COD: His windpipe's gone. I'm punching a hole so he can get some air.

(COD cuts into BRANDON's neck to make a hole so he can breathe. This is a medical procedure, and COD knows what he's doing.)

ROACH: Where are they?

COD: Keep his head back.

ROACH: Maggot!

(COD strips off his shirt to put it under BRANDON's head)

COD: It will help him breathe.

(COD has chest wraps underneath to hold down her breasts. COD is a woman. BRANDON tries again to speak.)

ROACH: Shut up. Don't talk.

(MAGGOT *enters. She sees* COD.)

MAGGOT: Jesus Christ.

COD: Have they shut down the mains?

ROACH: Ssshhhhh.

(ROACH *kisses* BRANDON, *gently on the mouth.*)

MAGGOT: I don't know.

ROACH: Stay with us.

(SAUSAGE MAN *slowly walks across the stage. Only* COD *sees him.* SAUSAGE MAN *kneels beside* BRANDON, *removes the knife, and gently blows into* BRANDON's *neck.* BRANDON *is dead.*)

(*End Scene Ten*)

Scene Eleven

(BAQUIN *in his office.* TUCK *paces back and forth.*)

TUCK: Damage is at a minimum. They were able to shut the down the mains within minutes.

BAQUIN: He should have been wearing safety equipment.

TUCK: We don't have any.

BAQUIN: Nonsense. I filled out an order.

TUCK: We've got no sprinkler system, most of the extinguishers are shot.

BAQUIN: That wasn't his job.

TUCK: Half the safety exit doors are bolted shut.

BAQUIN: The boy was out of line.

TUCK: He had the assignment.

BAQUIN: Call the insurance company. I want them to know that he wasn't wearing the required safety equipment.

TUCK: We don't have any safety equipment.

BAQUIN: He was careless.

TUCK: I changed three of those gauges myself two days ago. That ammonia is so cold in a liquid form and it touches you and it's like taking a lit match—

BAQUIN: The board is breathing down my neck.

TUCK: —tttssshhh—it will burn you that quick.

BAQUIN: Just make sure the papers know why it happened.

TUCK: Mr Baquin. *(Beat)* That's what it does in a vapor form in your lungs.

BAQUIN: I don't appreciate your *(Beat)* tone in this time of crisis. You've done well considering your...your beginnings, Buck. You've been given a chance—

TUCK: I earned—

BAQUIN: You earned? You've worked at opportunities offered by this company. The bottom line here, boy, is—

(BAQUIN holds out his hands to TUCK.)

BAQUIN: —don't bite the hands that feed you.

TUCK: *(He looks at BAQUIN's extended hands, then his own.)* See these hands?

BAQUIN: Look clean enough to—

TUCK: *(Interrupts)* Oh, they're clean enough. So clean I can't even see them anymore. I used to have hands. Good, strong, black hands that did what I told them to do. They were smart and skillful, good at whatever job I asked them to do. That didn't mean they still didn't complain and ache and bruise and bleed. They very near went for broke at some jobs. But they were mine, and they had a knowledge, a vocation, and when I went home at the end of the day, my hands went with me, and sometimes they played and strayed— strayed to other hands, caressed other hands, along and down and in between—

BAQUIN: Just what the hell do you—

TUCK: *(Interrupts)* Now I got this almighty position. Promotion: but no hands may apply. You know what my hands do now? They hold a clip board, or they hang at my side. And at the end of the day when I go home, I go home without them. *(Beat)* A man without hands. What do you think, Mr Baquin? On payday, how do you think he counts his change?

(BAQUIN is at a loss to answer TUCK. He stares at him for some uncomfortable moments.)

BAQUIN: I see. Yes. Well. I'm sorry. Now listen to me closely: if the papers pick up on that...that Cod character. Christ. This industry is bringing in the likes of him. Fire him. Her. Whatever.

TUCK: Cod can do the work of two men on the kill floor.

BAQUIN: A person like that shouldn't be handling meat. If the public gets a hold of this. It's unsanitary. It's unnatural.

TUCK: What's unnatural is that we figured she was a man so we started her off at the top. If we'd known she was a woman—

BAQUIN: *(Interrupts)* What are you saying? You've got to learn to articulate—

TUCK: *(Interrupts)* But what's really unnatural, Mr Baquin, is for a twenty-two-year-old boy to have his lungs burned out of his chest.

BAQUIN: A man like you needs to speak clearly, to have command—

TUCK: I changed three of those lines myself. It could've been me instead of him.

BAQUIN: Nonsense. You would have been wearing our safety equipment.

TUCK: That's the truth of it. It could've been anybody in this fucking packhouse. Anybody but you, 'cause you don't change lines. No. You'll never change lines.

(Suddenly, TUCK picks up the bowl with the snail in it and smashes it to the ground. BAQUIN remains calm. They look at the broken glass between them.)

(End Scene Eleven)

Scene Twelve

(MAGGOT, ROACH, and COD enter with heavy chains and begin to link these. At some point the SAUSAGE MAN will enter and watch them all from the shadows.)

COD: We could take this place over *after* the funeral.

ROACH: No. We do it now. Before they get wind of it and lock us out.

MAGGOT: I figured the next time we saw you it would be in a skirt.

COD: A girl can't chase a steer if she's wearing a skirt.

MAGGOT: *(Knocks COD over)* A girl can't chase a man if she's wearing a jockstrap.

COD: I don't wear a jockstrap.

MAGGOT: Well, thank God for that.

COD: Except when I go out on the town and want to make the effort.

ROACH: You are one confused girl.

COD: I've never been more certain.

MAGGOT: Get this, Roach: She was born from a corpse.

COD: I was born from a fire.

MAGGOT: You've been lying to us all this time. Pretending you were what you're not.

COD: You're the one who pretended.

ROACH: What's the matter, Maggot? She's got the same ass you were mooning about.

MAGGOT: *(Holds her knife to* COD'S *cheek)* So are you a bastard or a bitch?

COD: Depends on the job.

*(*SAUSAGE MAN *appears elsewhere on stage.)*

MAGGOT: You think you're something special?

(Makes a small cut on COD'S *cheek)*

MAGGOT: You bleed like the rest of us. *(She throws the knife down.)* That's for not thinking you could trust us.

COD: It wasn't a matter of trust.

MAGGOT: No, it was a matter of money.

COD: And a matter of balls. Working like a man, I feel more like a gal. Know what I mean?

ROACH: We've got eight minutes 'til we take over and lock ourselves in.

MAGGOT: Which changing room are you gonna use?

ROACH: Anybody that wants out better go now.

COD: Want to see a trick?

MAGGOT: I've seen enough.

COD: No you haven't. It's just beginning. *(Holds out her hand)* Go on. Touch me.

*(*MAGGOT *touches* COD'S *hand. A small flame erupts.* MAGGOT *jerks her hand back as though burned.)*

SAUSAGE MAN: I think it's time I took things back in hand.

*(*SAUSAGE MAN *exits.)*

ROACH: We got three minutes 'til we lock the doors. Help me with the chains!

*(*ROACH *collects the heavy chains.)*

MAGGOT: *(To* COD*)* Have you got the guts of a woman or a man?

COD: I've got guts. Years of them. More than enough for both of us.

MAGGOT: Then I dare you: take off your shirt.

COD: Really? What do I get in return?

MAGGOT: Name it.

COD: You knew what I was.

ROACH: Let's get on with it.

MAGGOT: I want to see if you've got the kind of chest I like.

COD: And what kind is that?

ROACH: One minute to lock.

MAGGOT: I'll know it when I see it.

(COD *strips off her shirt. She is still wearing the bandage.*)

ROACH: Forty-five seconds.

COD: Things aren't always the way you see it.

ROACH: *(Exiting with the last of the chains)* Thank God for that.

COD: Alright. You can look, but don't touch.

MAGGOT: What if I want to?

COD: You could get burned.

ROACH: Thirty seconds.

MAGGOT: That's what I want.

(COD *unwinds a piece of the bandage and hands it to* MAGGOT *who begins to circle* COD, *unwinding the bandage as* ROACH *counts down.*)

ROACH: *(Offstage)* Ten, nine, eight, seven,

MAGGOT: Six, five, four, three, two, one. Lock.

(*The bandage is unwrapped and drops to the floor. Now* MAGGOT *can see* COD's *breasts. At the same moment of revelation, we hear the deafening sound of many heavy doors being pulled shut and locking, continuous echoes of doors locking and locking.* MAGGOT *reaches out and touch's* COD's *breast. Then* MAGGOT *and* COD *kiss.*)

(*End Scene Twelve*)

Scene Thirteen

(BAQUIN *is alone and talking to himself.*)

BAQUIN: Tuck. You're a good man. I want you to go in there, right now, and check on our workers. Let me know what their mooooooooooo. Their mooooooooooooo. *(He stops speaking and begins to chew his cud much as a cow would.)* Oh, Tuck. My dear Tuck. Come back to me. You can't leave. Please, please, come back. It's lonely in here. The ultimate loneliness: to be the last of your kind.

(SAUSAGE MAN *enters.* BAQUIN *is startled.*)

BAQUIN: You're not Tuck.

SAUSAGE MAN: You're not happy making my sausages anymore.

BAQUIN: Oh, yes I am.

SAUSAGE MAN: No. You aren't. This is a terrible disappointment. Production has all but stopped. You see? (*He cranks his sausage machine.*) It's empty. I've run out of bits and pieces. No bits and pieces, no sausages.

BAQUIN: How can I help you?

SAUSAGE MAN: Get those doors open so we can move in there and crank things up again.

BAQUIN: It's out of my hands.

(SAUSAGE MAN *nears* BAQUIN, *who becomes nervous.* SAUSAGE MAN *steps on something, then looks at the bottom of his shoe.*)

BAQUIN: What's the matter?

SAUSAGE MAN: Looks like a bit of snot got stuck to my shoe.

BAQUIN: Oh no, oh no.

SAUSAGE MAN: Its time for a little intervention.

BAQUIN: The eternal night of extinction.

SAUSAGE MAN: Why, they've frightened you, haven't they?

BAQUIN: Nonsense. This strike is illegal. I'll call out the National Guard. (*Calls*) Tuck! Get in here. Tuck!

SAUSAGE MAN: Shhhh. I can see it's time. Time for some new blood. Would you like some grass?

(*He pulls some grass from his pockets and holds it out to* BAQUIN. SAUSAGE MAN *also reveals a cattle prod, which he hides behind his back.*)

BAQUIN: It's not my fault. That mob in there are tearing me limb from limb. They're cutting me to pieces. They're frying my bacon. The whole industry is being grilled to hell.

SAUSAGE MAN: It's fresh grass. I picked it myself.

(BAQUIN *sniffs the grass. Suddenly, he chomps at it, chews hungrily.*)

SAUSAGE MAN: That's it. That's it. Yes. They've been cutting you to pieces. I can see that. Into little tiny pieces that are so small no one will have any use for them. No one but me.

BAQUIN: Stay away from me.

SAUSAGE MAN: I can turn you into something useful.

BAQUIN: No, thank you. I'm not in the moooooooooooooooooooooooooooo.

(*He clears his throat but nothing else will come out but the sounds of a cow. He begins to chew his cud again.* SAUSAGE MAN *moves in on* BAQUIN *and begins to poke him with the cattle prod.*)

BAQUIN: Mooooooooooooooooo?

(BAQUIN's "moo" is cut short when he feels the charge of the cattle prod. SAUSAGE
MAN "herds" BAQUIN as they exit. The SAUSAGE MAN makes soft, little clucking
noises to encourage BAQUIN.)

SAUSAGE MAN: Yup...Yup....Yup, Yup.

(End Scene Thirteen)

Scene Fourteen

(Upstage, ROACH speaks to a murmuring crowd.)

ROACH: My friends. Welcome to Slaughter City. This is a place where things
go and go and go. Now, this is a place where things stop. Machinery stops.
Cows stop. Pigs stop. We stop. And, most importantly, the profits stop.
And, whenever the profits stop, things heat up fast. Brandon's death was
only the beginning. From now on, anything can happen. And we're going
to have to be ready for it.

(ROACH exits. COD enters from one side of the stage, and the SAUSAGE MAN
enters from the opposite side. BAQUIN's tie hangs from his grinder.)

SAUSAGE MAN: (He puts his grinder down in front of him.) I've been thinking
it over. You're right. Why play by the old rules? If you want to stay: okay.
Then it's the two of us here, together. Through to the bitter end. Who
knows? This might turn out to be the opportunity we've been waiting for.
But will both of us be here afterwards to mop up the mess? (He laughs with
true delight.) What a gamble! What a risk! I feel like my old self again.
As you said, sometimes history just isn't ready for you, so you give it—
(He lights a match.) —a shove.

(He drops the match into the top of the grinder and it makes a small flame.
COD stands watching, transfixed. She speaks as though in a trance.)

COD: I'm with the Knights of Labor.... No... With the United Mine...
(She shakes her head, trying to locate herself.) No. I know where I am.

(SAUSAGE MAN laughs.)

SAUSAGE MAN: (Sings) "Oh where, oh where can my little dog be?"

COD: I'm in a chicken processing plant. Somewhere in the broiler belt, in
1891... No. It was 1991.... A long time ago. Decades and decades from now.

SAUSAGE MAN: They died on the assembly line.

COD: Yes. That was in...Hamlet. In...South...in North Carolina.

SAUSAGE MAN: The chickens burned.

COD: The doors were chained shut. From the outside.

SAUSAGE MAN: Cluck. Cluck. Cluck. Mooooooooooooo.

COD: That was at the Triangle Shirt Waist Company.... A whole century from now. On the seventh... No! The chains were on the outside... No, no...The chains are on the inside. And this is somewhere else!

SAUSAGE MAN: This is nowhere else. And there was a fire.

COD: Yes. There was a fire.

SAUSAGE MAN: See you on the other side? *Bon voyage*, my friend.

(Split scene: The TEXTILE WORKER *is standing on the window ledge. She is dressed in a long, flowing dress from a time even before her time. A strange light lights her. She looks radiant.)*

COD: *(Throughout the following* COD *is still trying to locate herself.)* There was a fire.

TEXTILE WORKER: It started in a rag bin.

COD: On the seventh floor.

SAUSAGE MAN: The workers burned.

(The SAUSAGE MAN *moves away and watches* COD.)

COD: Yes. *(Beat)* No!

TEXTILE WORKER: And this is the eighth floor. I'm standing at the open window, and the heat is so big behind me that it's melting the dress off my back. My hair starts to burn. I know I'm going to jump. That way I'll have a few more seconds. Alive. *(Overlapping slightly with* COD*)* And I want—

TEXTILE WORKER & COD: —a few more seconds.

TEXTILE WORKER: Women are jumping out of the windows around me and below me, on the lower floors. From up here, they look like handkerchiefs falling to the ground.

SAUSAGE MAN: *(Making the sounds of a fire truck)* Ding, ding, ding.

COD: Yes. The fire trucks. In the distance.

TEXTILE WORKER: The ledge I'm standing on has started to burn under my feet. The soles of my shoes are gone. *(Beat)* I lean to jump, holding my belly where my four-month-old child is still alive within me, for a few seconds more. And then—*(The* SAUSAGE MAN *appears besides her.)*—he's there and he tells me:

SAUSAGE MAN: I can save your child.

COD: No!

TEXTILE WORKER: And I say yes, yes, and I make the promise:

SAUSAGE MAN: *(They chant the "promise".)* "If the child is my spark—

TEXTILE WORKER & COD: *(Slightly overlapping)* —forever and ever—

SAUSAGE MAN: —to light up the dark—

TEXTILE WORKER & COD: —whithersoever—

SAUSAGE MAN: —I choose to send her—

TEXTILE WORKER & SAUSAGE MAN: *(Chant together)* She'll live."

TEXTILE WORKER: And I agree to everything. Because I know her already. Because I want her to live.

COD: There was a fire.

TEXTILE WORKER: And then I jump.

SAUSAGE MAN: *(Angry now)* The workers burned!

COD: No! This is now. Not the day after. This is this hour.

TEXTILE WORKER: And in those seconds, with the wind rushing by me, tearing my dress from my body, I remember only one thing, being asked once, as a child: "If you had five seconds left to live—

COD: This hour.

TEXTILE WORKER: —what would you do?"

COD: I'm not going to leave.

TEXTILE WORKER: I didn't answer the question, because as a child I didn't know.

COD: We have to do something.... We have to.... Yes.

TEXTILE WORKER: But I know now. And so I do it.

COD: Because this is right now.

TEXTILE WORKER: I laugh.

COD: And it's...right here in front of....

TEXTILE WORKER: I laugh, because I feel her move inside me like a flame. *(She opens her arms as if to jump.)* I laugh, because I know she will never die.

COD: *(She has located herself. She shouts out, as though she were already somewhere else, as though her voice is crossing a great distance of time and place between herself and her fellow workers.)* Fire!

(For a moment we hear the sound of flames and burning. Then MAGGOT and ROACH rush in, having heard COD's shout of warning. ROACH and MAGGOT see the fire and move toward it to put it out. Now COD, MAGGOT, and ROACH use their aprons like blankets to try and put the fire out. The fire roars up brightly all around them as they continue fighting the fire. Then there is a blackout.)

END OF PLAY

THE WAR BOYS

ORIGINAL PRODUCTION

THE WAR BOYS had its first performance on 10 February 1993 at the Finborough Theater. The cast and creative contributors were:

Bradley Lavelle
Mathew Sharp
Ethan Flower

Director .... Kate Valentine
Design .... Fay Saxty
Music .... Alex Valentine

CHARACTERS & SETTING

GREG, *early twenties, Mexican-American, working class*
DAVID, *early twenties, college educated, privileged*
GEORGE, *early twenties, "home boy"*

TIME
Now

PLACE
At a place that could be the Mexico/Texas border

(The set is minimal and by no means "realistic". A part of a barbed wire fence, to suggest a "border", is visible. The three men enter the stage one at a time. Each one is carrying a heavy-duty spotlight. With a look of mutual consent they take up their positions. They're now going to "play" the War Boys game. They play this game for real. The three of them crouch on a raised area of the stage in silence, scanning the border, until DAVID points at something he sees moving out there.)

DAVID: Put the brights on. Now! Now!

(They turn their spotlights on toward the public.)

GEORGE: Fuckin' beaner. Look at him run!

DAVID: Sweet Christ, he's wearing my Adidas.

GEORGE: Call him down, Greg. He's slipping away.

GREG: This is car six of the War Boys. We got a slowrider sighted making for the crossing at fence line nine.

GEORGE: *(Grabs mike from GREG)* Should we go after him? Over. *(Listens)* Says he'll send a car over after he makes a stop at the ditch line.

DAVID: Dim them again.

(Lights are dimmed)

DAVID: I think we lost him. When he starts up the hill. Oh yes, yes, look at him sprint.

GEORGE: Ninja, ninja, ninja.

DAVID: Think I wasted four years at Stanford for nothing?

GREG: Shit. Shit. He's in reverse.

DAVID: Come back, Marlboro Man. Come back to the Marlboro Land!

GEORGE: Damn. We lost him.

GREG: He'll be back.

DAVID: *(To GREG)* How come you were late tonight? I like to start on time.

GREG: Sorry. Had to finish up at the library.

DAVID: Oh? Beating off on Chaucer again, hey, Greggie.

GEORGE: Who's she?

DAVID: The Wife of Bath, yeah, baby.

GEORGE: *(Hears something)* Hey, did you hear that?

GREG: Sure. Swabbin' floors I get a lot of time to read. *(Beat)* I saw the other guys. They're at five tonight.

DAVID: Well, we're stuck right here until ten, then line seventeen 'til midnight.

GEORGE: Hey, want to see a trick?

GREG: By the way, David, it's a known fact that rich boys beat off three point seven times more than poor boys. Know why? *(Holds up his hands to* DAVID'S *face)*

GEORGE: I can hold a cigarette with my dick.

GREG: Because guys like me haven't got, excuse me, I mean "ain't" got all that free, leisure, wack-wack time.

GEORGE: Can we make it an early night tonight? Little bro is sick again.

DAVID: He's always sick. Take the kid to the doctor for a change why don't you.

GEORGE: Nothing I can't cure.

DAVID: With T L C, huh, Georgia?

GEORGE: Why not? Think I haven't got it in me?

DAVID: *(Sniffs)* Smell that aroma? It's the feminine scent. I'm going to pick up its trail.

(DAVID snorts, then throws himself to the ground and begins to belly-crawl about the stage, searching for something across the "border". GEORGE *and* GREG *ignore him.)*

GEORGE: It's your go.

GREG: I'm not in the mood.

GEORGE: It's your go.

GREG: No thanks.

GEORGE: Come on. You promised. You played it with David last time.

(GEORGE rolls up his sleeve and after some moments, GREG *does so wearily. Then* GREG *slaps* GEORGE, *though not hard, across the face. As they converse.* GEORGE *returns the slap, somewhat harder. Each slaps the other harder until one of them loses their balance. Meanwhile,* DAVID *is still crawling about sniffing.)*

GREG: So who's our contact tonight?

(Slaps GEORGE)

GEORGE: Officer Sharons.

GREG: Shit. Sharons is a drunk ass. Always too slow on the call-up.

GEORGE: *(Slaps* GREG*)* He says there's a hole they're getting through somewhere from three through seven.

GREG: *(Slaps* GEORGE*)* There's always a hole.

GEORGE: You ever notice something funny about my smile, Greg? *(Slaps* GREG*)*

GREG: Ask me about your breath.

GEORGE: *(Slaps* GEORGE*)* No, boy. The smile.

(Grins hugely and holds it. GREG *slaps him hard.)*

GREG: Food. In the corner of your mouth. *(Slaps* GEORGE*)* Hear that? Listen.

GEORGE: What?

GREG: Listen.

GEORGE: I don't hear anything. *(Beat)* For a mop-boy you sure are stupid.

(Slaps him hard. GREG *is knocked off his seat.)*

GEORGE: It never lasts more than ten hits with you. You're a wimp.

DAVID: *(Still crawling about)* Psst. Here sissy, sissy, sissy.

GEORGE: I mean it. What kind of animal do I smile like?

GREG: A worm. How about a worm?

GEORGE: Hey, David, what was that fancy-ass word for chewing you used the other night?

DAVID: I see you. I see you.

GREG: Masticate.

GEORGE: Yeah. What animal do I masticate like? *(Chews loudly)*

DAVID: *(Whispers)* Come here. I won't hurt you.

GREG: A groundhog?

GEORGE: It's dead zone here.

*(*DAVID *circles back to their area, grabs* GREG's *leg and clings to him, exaggerating.)*

DAVID: Oh, Father, who art in heaven, help me to step down from this stifling perch. Help me to respect manual labor, so I can wear filthy overalls, so I can make money with my own bare hands and get out of those oppressive neighborhood recycling programs.

GEORGE: Let's move.

GREG: We've got to wait 'til ten.

(Shakes DAVID *off)*

GREG: Sorry, Buddy. Once an M C-er, always and M C-er.

GEORGE: What's an M C-er?

DAVID: Moose-Cuticle, you idiot.

GREG: Short for Middle Class.

DAVID: Go easy on him, Greg. He can only take a bit of learning at a time.

GEORGE: *(Baring his rear to* DAVID*)* Have a bite from my left cheek, Mr Diploma. *(Beat)* Hey, I've got a game we can play.

DAVID: *(Standing and composing himself. To* GEORGE:*)* Nope. We're going to play mine. *(To* GREG*)* I would like to bet you five dollars you can't, excuse my coarseness, jerk off while I'm saying the Pledge of Allegiance.

GEORGE: I bet I could.

DAVID: *(Still to* GREG*)* Five bucks you can't.

*(*GREG *ignores him.)*

GEORGE: *(Moves a good distance from them)* I'll do it over here.

DAVID: *(To* GEORGE*)* Nope, I'll need to see the evidence.

GREG: You two are kindergarten.

GEORGE: *(Moves closer)* O K, but no peeking.

DAVID: On your marks.

GREG: This is the last time I'm out with you two.

DAVID: Get set.

GREG: I just want to make that clear.

GEORGE: Go.

DAVID: I pledge allegiance to the flag, to the United States of America— *(He mimics a quarterback while he recites, both fast and slow.)* —and to the Republic for which it stands, one nation, under God, indivisible, with liberty and justice for all.

GEORGE: Start over.

DAVID: Five bucks. Now.

GEORGE: Fuck off. I already owe you two hundred and thirty.

DAVID: Now you owe me two hundred and thirty-five.

GEORGE: Yeah, well, I almost had you, bud. But when you got to the "and to the Republic" bit that brought me down.

DAVID: Your credit with me is going to drop, sir, if you can't improve your performance.

GREG: You two. Shit. *(Beat)* Listen, we stay in the car tonight or I'm quits with you guys.

GEORGE: *(To* GREG*)* Will you quit worrying?

GREG: I mean it.

GEORGE: We're friends, Greg. A promise is a promise.

DAVID: What about last Friday night? Standing on the sidelines observing it all. I could see it was tickling your palate.

GREG: *(Interrupts)* I was fucked up that night. I'm not like you dogs.

*(*DAVID *meows.)*

DAVID: But I polished my hood tonight especially.

GREG: Tonight we stay in the car and let the officers handle the rest.

DAVID: *(Pushing* GREG *with his finger)* Since when do you call the shots for this brigade? Hey? Who gives you a ride here in the evenings?

GREG: You do.

DAVID: Who pays for the gas?

GREG: You do.

DAVID: Who buys you your six-pack?

GREG: I just don't want things to get messy tonight.

GEORGE: Don't spoil the evening, Greg.

DAVID: Hey. I never swore I wasn't a sick individual now did I?

GEORGE: We'll be good. My bro's sick. I want to be home early. *(Gets on his knees and shouts towards the border, which is now the public)* Mama Mia. Come on, come on! Let's light this birthday cake!

DAVID: Hurry, hurry. Step right up. *(Kneels next to* GEORGE, *extends his arms to public)* See the greatest show on earth.

*(*GREG *now joins in. The tune for this song should give the sense of a chain-gang type ballad.)*

ALL: *(Border Song)*
On the border, we can see the pretty sights,
Some in the day, but the best ones at night
Bring a six-pack of Bud and a bag of chips
Bring some soda pop and some tamale dip.

We can spot them running, we can watch them crawl
We can tie them up, we can have a ball.
We can make ten dollars if we catch one alive
The Feds will pay us money and they'll give us no jive.

(DAVID *jumps up, toppling* GREG.)

DAVID: Shhhh. Did you hear that?

GEORGE: What?

GREG: Where?

DAVID: Shhhhh. *(Sings again, but alone, as others tap out music)*
Barbaric? A clear case of missing morality?
You're wrong, this fun's a duty from the highest authority
These beaners don't value life as we boys do
We heard it from the top, they want to mix a racial stew.

GREG: *(Sings)* Now we got dead-end jobs or the army option
We can travel to kill or we can sell the MacLuncheon.

GEORGE: *(Sings)* But why take orders or clean up someone's shit
When we can light up the border, ten dollars a hit.

DAVID: You know what I heard today? They say some of our own kind have
crossed over there.

(All three are on guard and nervous.)

GEORGE: Over there?

DAVID: Forming a so-called "protect the Mex" band. *(Beat)* Could be they're
carrying knives.

GREG: I don't think so.

DAVID: Could be they're carrying guns.

GEORGE: Guns?

GREG: Don't listen to him George.

DAVID: Scared, Greg?

GEORGE: Hey, I heard something.

DAVID: Shhhh. What was that?

GREG: George's gut.

DAVID: There it is again. Hear it?

(They all huddle.)

GEORGE: I heard it.

GREG: Shhhhh.

DAVID: Sounds like

GEORGE: Like

GREG: Like

DAVID: Like a knife sharpening on a stone.

GEORGE: *(Whispers)* Let's get out of here.

GREG: *(Whispers)* Just some stones rolling down the hill, George.

DAVID: *(Sees something)* What's that?

GEORGE: Where?

GREG: Where?

DAVID: Something shining. Two. Three things shining.

GEORGE: *(Whispers)* Let's go.

GREG: I don't see anything shining.

DAVID: *(Whispers)* Blades. Knife blades. *(Shouts)* Blades!

(As DAVID shouts he throws a knife in front of them, and GREG and GEORGE both scare and duck. Then DAVID is laughing at them.)

GEORGE: That's not very funny, David.

DAVID: With you two I can't resist.

GREG: *(Clutching his stomach)* Hold it.

DAVID: Must you repeat this performance every time there's a little excitment down here? I say "boo" and you puke.

(GREG moves upstage and begins to vomit.)

DAVID: Couldn't you get some pills to keep it down? You're pitiful, sweetheart.

GEORGE: *(Hands over ears)* That noise gets to me.

DAVID: Five bucks says I can make it worse for you, Greg.

(GREG is oblivious to them and continues being sick. GEORGE stands over him with his arm raised like the Statue of Liberty.)

DAVID: *(Sings)* America, America
God shed his grace on thee
And crown thy good
With brotherhood
From sea to shining sea

(As DAVID is still singing, GREG recovers and lights change slightly as he moves downstage right, near public, wiping his mouth on his sleeve.)

DAVID: You, my man, don't have the belly to take a joke.

GEORGE: Take it easy, Greg. He didn't see anything.

GREG: Yeah? Well, maybe I did.

(During GREG's *monologue,* GEORGE *and* DAVID *carry on in and around the car area.They are not unaware of* GREG's *performance, rather they are not really interested in it. At times, however, they will intervene.* GREG *is addressing the border here.)*

GREG: *(To border)* Hey! Hey! *Dame dos cuchillos.* Throw me a couple of knives. *(Turns back to his friends a moment)* Think I haven't got it in me? Maybe I'll just step over there and find out if they're carrying knives. *(Spits on his palms, smooths back his hair, addresses border again)* Think I haven't got it in me? Scared, are you? *(Beat)* Hey. I bet you never belonged to the Boy Scouts. I did. The church choir? *(Holds a note)* I could hold the longest note. Then I went on to join the Sunday Dixie Band. And then the Blueshell Campaign to save the farmers. Then I joined the Border Brigade. *(Lifts his shirt and draws an imaginary line down the center of his body)* This half of me is Mejicano. This other half of me is WASP. *Como sabes* which side is which? My mother was Mexican. She used to tell me: "*Este lado es Mejicano.* This side is Mexican— *(Slaps left breast)* —the side with the heart."

GEORGE: *(Spots something)* Look.

DAVID: Another one!

GEORGE: A beaner chick. In heat.

GREG: My father *me dijo* it was my lower half that was WASP, that I had his *cojones*— *(Grabs crotch)* —but the brains of a beaner. *(Beat)* When I was a little nino I was two separate pieces, just below the surface, held together by skin.

DAVID: Here she comes.

GEORGE: Throw the brights on her.

DAVID: Not yet, not yet. Wait.

GREG: Didn't do sports. Didn't run during recess. Never got on a bike. *Nada ni mierda.* If I'd made the wrong move I'd split, right down the center.

DAVID: You're missing the spectacle, Greggie.

GEORGE: Open the sun roof. Hey, baby. Slip under the wire.

DAVID: We're the Holiday Inn.

GEORGE: The Light Up the Border Brigade.

GREG: *Mi padre,* he was a Senior *Agente* of the Border. He used to take a lot of slack for having married a Wet. But he always said it was strategy, that he knew them better, inside and out, on account of her.

DAVID: Come and get your red, hot one-hundred-percent American hard-on.

GEORGE: *(Sings)* It's the real thing...

GREG: They say he was a good cop.

DAVID: *(Sings)* That's the way it should be....

GREG: He made O K *dinero*, helped me get a loan so I could get my first car. Then I met my first girl. She was Chicana. *(Beat)* I figured, like father, like son. And this *chica* was legal, nice trailer, two-parent family. She wasn't real pretty, but she gave me a feeling *(Beat)* like eatin' a bowl of frosted flakes with tequila. We were planning on living together, so I brought her home to meet my father.

DAVID: Look at that.

GEORGE: She's stuck.

DAVID: Her shirt's tangled up in the wire.

GREG: He called us into his office. I told him I was thinking about marrying her. He took a hold of Evalina's long braid and tipped her head back. *(Beat)* Then he stuck his fingers in her mouth and tested her molars. He found the hole where she'd just had a tooth pulled. He jammed his nail in it, and she yelled. Then he just shook his head. He was disappointed.

GEORGE: She can't get loose.

GREG: Then he took out his wallet. "You can't marry a woman with a bad set of teeth," he said. "It spoils the breath." He counted it out: *veinte, quarenta, sesenta, cien.* Two hundred bucks.

DAVID: Come on, Godiva. A few more shakes, and I'll let you polish the hood of my new mustang.

GREG: My Evalina was wearing an orange blouse that day, with a blue ribbon braided into her hair.

DAVID: But she doesn't even look Mexican.

GEORGE: Maybe she's Arab.

GREG: He unbuttoned her blouse and tucked the money in her bra. *(Beat)* Then he kissed us both on the forehead.

DAVID: *(Shoving him)* Go on, George. Talk to her.

GEORGE: But I can't speak Spanish.

DAVID: Shit Spanish. She's a bitch. Give her poetry.

GREG: Over breakfast the next morning he asked me if I'd made the appointment with the dentist.

GEORGE: *Chica, chica.*

GREG: I said yes. I told him me and Evalina, we both appreciated his advice.

DAVID: Not that. Marvell, stupid. Watch this: "When as in silks my...beaner goes, then, then, methinks how sweetly flows the greasafaction of her clothes. Next when I cast mine..."

GEORGE: It worked. She's grinnin' like a raccoon. Hey, hamburguesa!

GREG: I suppose Evalina went and got her teeth fixed. I don't know. She wouldn't see me after that.

DAVID: This is America. Over ninety billion served.

GREG: I mean, *mi padre*, he was a strict man sometimes, but he looked out for me.

GEORGE: Move over. Let me out of the car.

GREG: *(To* GEORGE *and* DAVID, *who have begun to encroach too far on his story)* Stay in the fuckin' car, George.

GEORGE: The lady needs to be rescued. *(To* DAVID*)* Just watch this. You watching?

GREG: Asshole. We've got a deal with the Feds. We spot them. That's all. If we fuck up again...

GEORGE: Fuck you, Greg. Hey, *muchacha*!!

DAVID: Look at old Georgie. He's combing back his hair.

GREG: You two baboon asses are fuckin' up my thing.

(Pushes GEORGE *back)*

GREG: Can't you shut up just a few more seconds until I'm done?

*(*GEORGE *and* DAVID *mock-freeze. For some seconds* GREG *doesn't know where to pick up again.)*

GREG: I suppose Evalina got her teeth fixed. I don't know. She wouldn't see me after that...

DAVID: *(Interrupts)* No, no. You left off at *(Mocks* GREG'S *voice)* "He was a strict man, but he looked out for me."

GREG: Yeah. Thanks. *(Beat)* But he looked out for me. It was about a year later, and I came home to visit my mother. I told her about me and Evalina being over, about how Father had offered to pay to fix her teeth. I watched her pour a whole bottle of detergent into the washer. Then she said, like she might have been saying "hand me a towel", "And you let him do that?" *(Beat)* Then she smacked me across the face. Not hard. But it was the first time she ever hit me. Then she just kept saying it, over and over: "*Y lo dejaste hacerlo?*" And you let him do that?

DAVID: *(Louder)* And you let him do that?

GEORGE: *(Louder)* And you let him do that?

GREG: I almost said, "She was just a fuckin' beaner, Ma." *(Begins to laugh)* Wouldn't have been the appropriate thing to say. When my father walked through the door that night, "bang", she hit him over the head with a dinner plate. *(Raises arms slowly as though holding a gun and fires)* Bang... bang...bang...A few years later, my father *se murio*. Dead. I dragged around the half of me *que fue muerte*, his dead half. Sometimes I'd wake up in the middle of the night and I'd smell its deadness, like rotten cantaloupe. *(Beat)* So that's why I joined up. Because, even though my mother died shortly after, the beaner half of me wouldn't die.

DAVID: Hold it!

(He hurries over and lifts up GREG's foot.)

Look at this. You're standing on a sapling. How many times do I have to tell you to watch where the hell you're standing. Lucky you didn't break the poor little fellow's back. Go stand somewhere else.

(GREG moves a few feet away.)

GREG: Here?

(DAVID motions with his hand for GREG to move a little farther.)

GREG: Here?

(DAVID nods O K and returns to the car. GREG continues)

GREG: As a matter of fact, the beaner half of me began to move in on the other half. In no time at all I was seventy-percent beaner, and it keeps spreading. Before I know it, *uno, dos, tres*, I'll be a hundred-percent pure beef wetback. I'm feeling it in my bones. And my feet, they want to dance that cockroach song. *(Does a mild tapdance of sorts)* But every time we catch one of those Mejicanos crossing the border, the pressure eases up. *Y puedo descansar.*

DAVID: Look, George. She's still there. Waiting.

GEORGE: *(Approaching public as though it were the girl)* Hey, Snow White. Want a bite of my apple?

GREG: *(Continues)* The creeping flow of her blood in me backs up a bit, and I can rest for a while—

DAVID: That-a-boy, Georgie. Show her your intellect.

GREG: —and stop fighting it. *(Beat)* So I hunt. It's harmless, really.
(Strums barbed wire again and sings, to the tune of "Oh, Susannah")
Oh, Evalina, no llores mas por mi
(Stops, then starts again in English)
Oh Evalina, don't you cry for me
For I'm going on down to the border
With a six pack cross my knee.
(Laughs self-consciously, then speaks nervously to DAVID as he nears the car area)

Make him get back in the car. She could pull a knife on him. *(To public again)* I try not to hurt them, though, especially the women.

DAVID: It's just like watching your V H S.

GREG: It's nothing personal. I mean, I loved my mother and she was one of them. *(To his friends)* Shit, come on, you guys. This isn't part of the deal. Can't you wait until I'm done?

(GEORGE gazes across the public then begins to crawl closer as he "sees" the woman nearing the border.)

DAVID: What's the matter, Greggie? Not getting the attention you need?

GREG: *(Tries to get back to his story)* Especialmente las mujeres, the women. Just want to *espantarlos un poco*, scare them up a bit, let them know they don't belong here. And we get ten bucks for each one we catch. In a good week I can make seventy, eighty bucks. Helps on the bills.

DAVID: Get lucky, baby. Heads or tails.

GREG: But, hey, let's lighten up now. *Vengan. Vengan.* Loosen up. We'll pick up a bottle of rotgut tequila, cruise on down to Dairy Mart road and shine the brights on the wire, light 'em up, catch us some fish, some *peces* for supper, huh?

(Huge groan from DAVID in the car. GREG is disconcerted a moment.)

(To DAVID) Fuck off. *(Beat)* I mean, we're all a mix, aren't we? *(Whispers)* But which half has got the heart, huh? Huh?

DAVID: Hey, Greg, how do you spell relief?

GREG: *(Oblivious to DAVID's interference)* Come on. You can get some relief. Take your mind off of a long day's work.

DAVID: Well?

GREG: *(To public)* So how do you spell relief?

(GEORGE begins to caress the stage floor as he stares out at the woman that we can't see. He does this sensually, carefully.)

DAVID: *(To GEORGE)* I spell it B-E-A-N-E-R-S.

GREG: Beaners.

(GREG jumps back in the car.)

DAVID: George will teach her the lesson she needs. She'll run back home now, tell her compadres: "You're playin' with fire, and you can be burned by fire...." *(To GEORGE)* What's the rest of the pledge, George? I'll knock ten dollars off your tab if you can remember it.

GEORGE: *(Remembering)* It goes... It goes... "can be burned by fire...and the...the...white man will rub two Mexicans together to make his fire."

GREG: *(Interrupts)* That's it. I'm walking. Get out of my fuckin' way.

DAVID: *(Grabs GREG by collar)* But old Ronald McDonald is going to score ninety billion and one tonight.

GREG: I'm calling Sharons.

DAVID: Can you smell the meat cooking, Greggie? Or are you going to spoil your appetite again? *(Beat)* Hey, give me that radio, you—

GREG: Calling for Officer Sharons. Calling for Officer—

DAVID: You idiot!

GREG: Emergency. A dozen beaners just broke the line at fence number—

(DAVID hits GREG across the face with his gun.)

GREG: Fuck! You busted my goddamn nose.

DAVID: What has gotten into you?

GREG: I don't want things getting out of hand.

DAVID: You didn't mind things getting out of hand the other night, though, did you?

GREG: That was different. This one's a kid.

DAVID: Sure, sure. Old Greggie coaching on the sidelines. Grunt, grunt, grunt.

GREG: *(Motioning to gun)* O K. But you said you'd leave that at home tonight. Give it to me.

DAVID: *(Calmly)* But it's my toy, Greg. And this is my car. As a matter of fact, this is my brigade. I got us the deal with the Feds, didn't I? Ten dollars a tag, remember?

GREG: Get back in the fuckin' car, George.

DAVID: You're not very appreciative, Greg. I don't like that in a man.

GREG: George!

DAVID: This is disappointing me, Greg.

GREG: We made a deal with the Feds we wouldn't touch them anymore.

DAVID: George!

GEORGE: What? What? O K. Everything's cool. Don't get upset, Greg. *(Turns)* Look, she's fine. There she goes. I didn't touch her.

DAVID: Runnin' on back to Disneyland.

GEORGE: See? We can keep things in hand. It's cool.

GREG: Let's get out of here. This night is cracked.

GEORGE: Sure. Anything you say, Greg. We're all friends here, right?

GREG: Look. I want to have a good time too. Why do you two always have to fuck up my show?

DAVID: We'll be good little gentlemen from now on. Trust us, Greg.

GEORGE: Yeah. Trust us.

DAVID: *(Sneering)* And I apologize for slapping you. Really.

(Suddenly, DAVID throws himself on GEORGE's shoulder and begins, we think, to weep. GREG and GEORGE watch with concern. GEORGE is fooled.)

GEORGE: He's choked up.

DAVID: *(Through his gasping)* "This side is Mexican...the side with the heart..." Such a touching story, Greg.

GREG: Not bad, eh?

DAVID: There were times I thought I heard angels singing between the lines. *(Beat)* I mean, you're O K, Greg. *(Beat)* So, if it came down to it, down to the nitty-gritty, which would you choose, Birdseye's or Stouffer's?

GREG: I'm a canned foods man myself.

GEORGE: What's with the canned foods?

GREG: Shut up, George.

GEORGE: No.

DAVID: *(To GEORGE)* Take his advice, son, or you'll get your feelings hurt. *(To GREG)* Well?

GREG: Well?

GEORGE: Hey, I can make a balloon with my spit. *(He blows spit bubbles.)*

DAVID: Did they go for it?

GREG: I'm not sure.

DAVID: You're not sure? Every soldier must be sure.

GREG: That's right. No uncertainty. No doubts.

GEORGE: Come on, Greg. Is that true, the bit about your Dad and her molars?

GREG: Yep. But I threw in the part about him unbuttoning her shirt.

DAVID: So you fabricated?

GREG: Only in a minor way.

GEORGE: And your Dad, beaned to death with a dinner plate?

GREG: Nope. Cholesterol got him.

DAVID: He should have borrowed my rowing machine. *(Beat)* Shhh. Hear that, George?

(GEORGE shakes his head "no" while he listens.)

DAVID: Sounded like a howl.

GREG: No, David. You're a howl.

DAVID: That's the border wolf. It howls like that just before it kills.

GEORGE: I didn't hear a howl.

GREG: *(Joining in to get GEORGE)* I did. It sounded like this.

(GREG springs up on car and howls. This should be more frightening than funny.)

GREG: Well, how did I do?

DAVID: One minor criticism: your prose is a tad flat, somewhat backwards, too...working class. You've got to flex it up a bit.

GREG: You think so?

GEORGE: Can we quit early tonight? I need to call little bro.

DAVID: I'm sorry about Evalina.

GREG: Thanks.

DAVID: She was always nice to me when I came by your place for dinner. Once, she wiped the corners of my mouth with her apron. I think she appreciated my appetite. I always had a third helping.

GREG: You never met Evalina.

DAVID: You see how you restrict your imagination?

GEORGE: He's probably waiting up for me.

GREG: My imagination?

GEORGE: It's a nice thing to have someone waiting up for you.

GREG: *(Poking DAVID with his finger)* All you're good at is giving points, Mr Critic. Why don't you go stand out over there and see how many knives you can catch with your teeth. I caught three myself.

DAVID: Tsk, tsk. Do I detect a challenge? How infantile. But alright. *(He takes a dramatic breath, steps away from the car and faces the public.)* Alright. *(Calls)* Hello? Anyone at home? I know you're out there. And I'm calling especially to you sweet Yankee blue-bloods who belong on this side, not that one.... Look, I am going to give you a target, right inside here. *(He opens his mouth wide and hisses for some moments.)* Throw them right in here. Right in the bullseye. Or how about this? *(He turns his back to the public, spreads his arms and legs.)* Aim for the spine. Go ahead. Give me a tickle. *(Beat)* They're not interested in me, Greg. It's you they're lusting for. See? They won't tickle with me. *(Beat)* Alright then. *(Spins around)* Then I'll tickle with you. *(Beat)* Want to see me do an imitation of a baby radish with its roots growing?

GREG: A radish *is* a root.

DAVID: But the root has got roots as well and they crawl deep in the dark, like this.

(DAVID squirms about. He is serious about doing a good imitation. He begins to make hissing sounds also. GREG and GEORGE remain in or around the car area.)

DAVID: Listen! Listen! You can hear them growing...radish roots. They make a sound when they grow— *(Makes a sound)* —radiating out minute bits of heat into the wet dirt, making the wet dirt hiss. *(Makes hissing noises)* Hot in the mouth! The tongue burning. My sister and I. We'd fill up our mouths, see who could chew up the most before we spit them out like confetti, all over our shoes. *(Beat)* When my mother tried to leave, I said to her: "Mother, you're an insect, and, like the child you brought me up to be, I'll pluck out your wings." *(Beat)* After Sis passed away, I couldn't apologize about the radishes. I had wanted to send Sis a nice card, some chocolates, maybe a balloon. She was an intelligent girl. When she left home, she said to me: "I'm root-bound here. And now I've got to crack my pot." *(Laughs nervously)* Telephone pole cracked her pot too, you could say. *(Pretends to write a letter in the air)*

GREG: *(Sees a child in the distance)* Check this out: a toddler.

GEORGE: *(Yells)* Hey, kiddo, *(Whistles)* want to play Master of the Universe?

DAVID: Dear Sis: Sorry about the radishes. Love, Bro. *(Takes off his shoe, polishes it on his thigh, and carefully lines it up on the stage floor)*

GREG: Nope. Headin' his fanny back to them hills.

GEORGE: *(Motioning towards DAVID)* He's strippin' again.

GREG: This is getting to be a yawn, David.

DAVID: *(Ignoring them)* Now, my mother was what you might call a...call a... *(Snaps his fingers until his friends give him his line)*

GREG: ...a dignified type.

DAVID: *(Continues)* ...call a...dignified type of insect, like the mantis. Her wings. Just wouldn't give, not matter how hard you tugged. One day my mother is making me P B J's three stacks high. The next day she's taking off her apron, balling it up, shoving it down the compactor, walking out. When I tackled her on the lawn, asked her why, she said I was old enough to take care of myself, that she was growing weary of the sight of me. She gave me a look then, the way a hole looks back at you if you're looking down in it. And then I knew she knew about Sis. *(Takes off other shoe, polishes it, and lines it up carefully next to the other one)*

DAVID: My Daddy had a saying: Never...Never... *(He can't remember his lines.)* Fuck!

GREG: Never shut your eyes.

DAVID: Never shut your eyes to a woman...because if you do, before you know it, she'll stick you full like a pin cushion, sew your scrotum to your ass, use you for a foot stool. *(Takes off one sock, lays it gently beside a shoe)* Radishes. A shame they ever existed. *(Beat)* I could have plucked out their wings like insects. But they wouldn't. Stand still. They squirm. They wiggle. They wreak havoc in your garden. *(Removes other sock. Notices bare feet and wiggles them in fascination.)* Hey. You got to keep fit. If the body is a drag... *(Snaps fingers. No response. Snaps them again.)*

GREG: Learn the shit, will you, David.

DAVID: Show some consideration, please?

GREG: *(Wearily)* If the body is a drag, the spirit's gonna— *(Sticks his finger in his mouth and gags)*

DAVID: —the spirit will gag. *(Sits down and begins to row)*
Row, row, row your boat
Gently down the stream
Merrily, merrily, merrily, merrily
Life is but a
(Draws out last note)
Radish!
(Quits rowing. Gets up and unbuttons his shirt.)

GEORGE: *(To GREG)* How much you think they're paying for this peep show?

DAVID: I mean, when you grow up you've got choices to make in life. So you choose: Johnny Carson or Hee-Haw, Seven-Up or Sprite, C B S or N B C, Beechnut or Juicy Fruit, Trident or Dentine. *(Beat)* I had a fiancée once. But every time I desired her and leaned to deliver the first real kiss of my life, this music began in my ear *(Sings)*:

Wrigley Spearmint gum, gum, gum
Wrigley Spearmint gum, gum, gum

(As he repeats these lines, GREG and GEORGE sing the accompaniment to the song "Carry it with you...That great fresh flavor" until DAVID silences them with his arms, as a conductor of an orchestra would.)

DAVID: Excuse me, gentlemen, but I like to do it solo. *(Beat)* Somehow the melody put me off kissing her. Or I'd reach in her shirt to fondle her breast and whisper bits of sassyfras into her ear, but instead I'd start *(Sings)*
Gettin' that barefoot feelin'
Drinkin' Mountain Dew
(Laughs wildly as though tickled. Then speaks seriously.)

When things get hot, cool is all you got. *(Beat)* I couldn't get that music out of my brain. *(Beat)* I work for a law firm. *(Lays shirt out on floor and kneels to button it up again)* My partner says he likes girls in their adolescence. My father liked them young too, but he swore sheep had the greater dignity. He brought a girl home for me once when I made an A in Mathematics. And the three of us got drunk. *(Laughs)* All I remember are three white hooves and one black one. *(Stands and sings in opera style)*
Baa-baa black sheep
Can I tickle your wool?
I've only been arrested once. After Sis's funeral. I went out hacking up neighbor's gardens, hunting for radishes. This officer picked me up, along with this Chicano teen from downtown. At the jail he thought I'd passed out. She was fighting like a whirlwind, so he put a gag on her in the cell adjacent to mine and pulled off her trousers. I could see the girl's face. She was trying to scream, but the gag wouldn't let her. The officer was so busy with her he didn't see me reach my arm through the bars and touch her face. She had hair that curled like Sis's. Come on, I whispered to her, scream, scream, damn you. And her whole face was screaming, only no sound was coming out, and I felt like someone pulled my plug, because I started to scream instead: *(Whispers)* No! No! and I kept on screaming until the officer put out my lights.

GREG: There! George! There's two of them!

GEORGE: Where? I can't see anything.

GREG: Right there! Look... Nope. Lost them. Damn.

DAVID: Then I dreamt about Sis, both of us up to our wrists in the dirt, fishing for radishes in the garden. Like a pearl in an oyster, she'd say, when she pulled one up out of the dirt. *(Beat)*....She was my...my.... *(Snaps fingers. No response.)* Hey!

GEORGE & GREG: Fuck you!

DAVID: She was my...friend. *(Takes off britches, lays them out. The shape of a person is now laid out on the floor.)*

GREG: Not the all-cotton Armani trousers.

DAVID: *(Playfully)* Now, which one is me? This one? *(To self)* or that one? *(To suit on floor)* Or is that old Sis lying there? *(Beat)* Sis and I were from an aspiring middle class neighborhood. Even as kids we were smart enough to keep our eyes on the next rung of the ladder.

(While DAVID tells the following, GEORGE crawls into DAVID's space, climbs onto the clothes and does push-ups over them.)

DAVID: Naturally, we hung around the top of the cream neighborhood parks so we could mingle with the best. I mean, in our town we were the "betters", but we aspired to be the best. Well, some of the kids we met there started calling me a pussy for hanging out with my sister. I was twelve and she was ten. They said I could join their club but that I'd have to choose, them or her. Of course I said I'd choose them, because I knew I could make it up to Sis later when we got home.

(Now GEORGE *flips over on his back and is motionless.* DAVID *stands over him.)*

DAVID: But then they gave me a dare in order to join. And they held her down.

(Kneels over GEORGE's *body.* GEORGE *is lifeless.)*

DAVID: They pulled up her skirt. They dared me. If you say no to a dare, you're a pussy. I could not be a pussy. But everything was getting sort of out of focus. I took the radishes out of my pocket. I had three of them, big as chestnuts that she and I dug that morning. I put them inside her.

*(*DAVID *kicks* GEORGE *hard in the side, but he does this with no apparent emotion.)*

DAVID: I put them inside her. She just kept whispering my name. She wouldn't scream. Just saying, *(Whispers)* "David, no. David, no. David, no. David, no."

*(*GEORGE *moves out of* DAVID's *"show".)*

DAVID: She never looked me in the face again, for eleven years, until her Toyota hit that telephone post. Then she had to look at me. Lying in that coffin, she had no choice but to look up at me. *(Speaks to clothes on floor)* "I'm sorry, Sis", I said. *(Speaks each word in isolation)* I am sorry. *(After a moment, spits on the face of the clothes figure on the stage floor. But this action is almost tender.)* Insects. Insects we were. And they plucked out our wings. *(Beat)* I'm not pulling your leg like Greg was. See, when you break a human being in half, right over your knee, crack, like a stick, there is no fixing him. Like there was no fixing her, my little sis.

(Covers face with hands as in a moment of agony, but then he is laughing. GREG *walks into* DAVID's *space.)*

GREG: Come on, come on. *Rapido, rapido.* "Bingo," goes *la cabeza*: David, you knock off wets for a kick, because you feel guilty about the...let's call it the vegetable rape of your *pobre hermana*. Go ahead, put yourself in the frame. Frame the pig.

DAVID: It was misplaced anger, transfer of violence, all due to a dysfunctional home.

GREG: It feels better, doesn't it, once you get a handle on the *problema*?

DAVID: I appreciate the kindness, Greg, but get the sweet Jesus out of my gig.

GREG: *(Returning to car)* You're not living up to your degree, David.

DAVID: Certainly I am *(Beat)* regretful about Sis. *(Makes popping sounds)* Fried my soul. But it isn't her at all. I'm tired of my job at the law firm. I'm bored. *(Beat)* There are just too many decisions to make: Mustard vinaigrette or the house special? B M W or Volvo? Paper or plastic?

(DAVID suddenly gags and begins to choke. GREG watches with disdain, but GEORGE is fooled. He cautiously approaches DAVID while glancing with fear at border.)

GEORGE: *(Whispers)* David?

(DAVID continues to gag.)

GEORGE: David? Are you O K? *(To GREG)* Something's the matter with him, Greg. Come and look.

(GEORGE touches DAVID with his foot. DAVID doesn't move. Then, suddenly, he grabs GEORGE's leg and bites it. GEORGE screams and shakes him loose. GREG and DAVID laugh together. Then DAVID looks around him.)

DAVID: Oh, no. Did I fall on my sapling?

GREG: I hope so.

GEORGE: That wasn't funny. I'm going home. Even if I have to walk.

(DAVID gets up and approaches GEORGE. DAVID spits on his hands and smooths GEORGE's hair back in place. This is a tender action. Then he suddenly strikes him.)

GEORGE: Hey!

DAVID: Remember our agreement? The three of us stick together. Right, George? Right?

(GEORGE doesn't answer.)

GREG: Lay off him.

DAVID: What?

GREG: I said lay off him.

DAVID: What did Greg say?

GREG: Greg said "Fuck you."

DAVID: *(Takes a moment to register this, then sings at GREG)*
On the border, Greg's getting nauseous.
On the border, he's just too serious.

GREG: *(Pushing DAVID backwards with the lines that he sings)*
On the border, you're playing frat-boy-king.
On the border, your education's nothing.

DAVID: *(Pushes Greg back with his lines as he sings)*
On the border, it's your American half-dream
One side upriver, the other downstream.

GREG: *(GREG is winning)*
On the border, too many tricks in your head
On the border, you just might wind up dead.

(There is a silence for some moments as GREG and GEORGE stare at one another. Then GEORGE begins applauding and continues until he gets their attention. Then DAVID grins and casually picks his clothes up off the floor and slings over his shoulder. He crosses to the car and GREG follows him.)

GEORGE: What a show!

DAVID: You liked that, didn't you?

GREG: I'd never have guessed.

GEORGE: You are a poet.

DAVID: Ah, but a poet born from grief. And everyone believes a poet, especially a poet who...

GEORGE: I had to memorize a poem once for class.

DAVID: ...indulges a little, elaborates a bit for the show.

GEORGE: Want to hear me recite it?

GREG: So the radishes were only an elaboration?

DAVID: Only an elaboration?

GEORGE: The poem I learnt was about an idiot who sawed off his arm.

GREG: So you lied.

DAVID: The radish episode is true.

GEORGE: I just got to say that that was a pretty disgusting thing to do to your sister, David.

(DAVID shrugs.)

GREG: I'm sorry about your sister. She always had a nice word for me.

DAVID: *(Casually)* You never met her.

(GREG shrugs.)

GEORGE: Do you think they're sorry?

(Motions to border)

DAVID: *(Whispers)* Frankly, dear, I don't give a damn.

GREG: So what did you choose in the end?

DAVID: Why, I choose Marlboro, Of course.

(DAVID *and* GREG *laugh together, as though to an inside joke.*)

GEORGE: *(Angered)* You two are so cool, aren't you? Big jokers with broken hearts.

DAVID: *(Looking at his watch)* It's time to move fence lines.

GREG: Yep. *Los peces* aren't biting here.

GEORGE: Well, I can do it too, you know.

DAVID: You've got asparagus for brains, Georgie. I said let's go.

GEORGE: You just watch. Old George will surprise you. *(He moves across stage, whistling and glancing shyly at the border/public.)*

DAVID: *(Claps softly)* That was wonderful, George, now zip your fly and let's go.

GEORGE: *(Confiding)* But it's different for me, 'cause mine is a secret.

DAVID: George. Old buddy. You're just blocking the view.

GREG: Shhh. George has a secret. Mustn't tell. Mustn't tell.

DAVID: Alright. But there's nothing that long-toothed border wolf hates more than a pitiful performance.

(GREG *and* DAVID *howl.*)

GEORGE: Just ignore them. *(Beat)* Lookie what I can do? *(Grabs barbed wire and twists it. Holds his hands up.)* See? *(Beat)* You got to forgive them. They want to be honest. They're O K guys. I grew up with them.

DAVID: This is a warning, George. If you step on that sapling... Move it. To the right.

(GEORGE *does so.*)

DAVID: Farther. Farther.

GREG: Farther.

GEORGE: *(Moves closer to public)* Is this O K? *(Beat)* I don't want them to hear some of this, so I got to speak soft. I was a kid when it started growing. It was the size of a penny, right in the middle of my back. It just popped up one day when I was standing in front of this billboard waiting for the school bus. On the billboard was a picture of a camel, sitting on a beach with sunglasses, smoking a cigarette. The camel had this smile on his face I'd never seen on any human face before: this smile of slap-happiness, of some just-do-it secret. And that's when I felt it pop up on my back: the hump. The camel's hump. *(Does a curious rotating motion with his shoulders)* Most kids would have got scared, but I wasn't surprised. I just kept it hid under my jacket so as not to scare my friends. *(Beat)* By the time I was a grown man I had a genuine camel's hump on my back.

GREG: His fuckin' hump again.

GEORGE: When it quit growing I started waiting in front of the mirror for the rest of it, for the smile. I was patient, too. But it didn't come. I started smokin' two at a time, to hurry it up a bit but the smile still held out on me. So there I was, a camel's hump without a smile, like a dick without balls. *(Itches his back)* Don't believe me? *(Turns around and lifts his shirt. We see nothing.)* Then what the hell is that? A pimple the size of a pup?

DAVID: It's an infected pore.

GREG: Another stripper. Yawn.

DAVID: Hey! Look out. I saw something move over there.

GEORGE: *(Pulls down shirt fast)* Don't touch. It's *my* hump. *(Beat)* Now my Daddy, he had—

DAVID: Not another father story.

GEORGE: —no hump, no smile, and, after the mines, only one lung to smoke with. But he was a G-O-O-D man. *(Beat)* I was into four-legged animals back then, so he took me hunting. I was seven. We sat on the tail of the truck, oiling the rifles. It was so cold I couldn't feel my hands in my gloves. I walked behind him. I must have stepped on every damn twig in the woods. He kept smacking the cap off my head— *(Smacks self in head a few times)* —telling me to shush up. Finally, we saw one. A buck. He was the size of a horse with antlers like Christmas trees. *(Dramatically)* His breath circled up out of his nose like ropes. *(Snickers at friends in car area)* Not bad, huh?

DAVID: George, I sense another boredom riot. If you don't pick up the rhythm, we might have to cancel. How about a questionnaire to liven things up? Let's see a show of hands. How many of you have enjoyed—

GEORGE: Shut up.

DAVID: *(Continues)* —a Big Mac so conscientiously that you had to hurry off to the restroom after the meal to beat off?

(Not to be discouraged, GEORGE returns to his monologue)

GEORGE: My Daddy whispered : *(Shouts)* "If you make a noise, I'll kill you." The barrel rose over my.... No... How about this: The cold, black barrel rose over my Daddy's shoulder—

DAVID: *(As though counting hands)* Which of you had the guts to switch from Coke to Pepsi out of respect for Schwarzkopf?

(GEORGE now raises the invisible rifle and aims it at his friends.)

GEORGE: —and he took aim. The buck raised its head. Its long tongue licked its grey nose. And then I saw it. *(Does so)* Wham. For the second, maybe last time in my life, that smile, that smirk of oblivion and party time. And then it hit me: That was my camel. Not a buck but my camel. *(Lets out a wild yodel)* That's just what I did. Then that camel burned rubber. The shot rang out. My father spun, and out went my lights.

GREG: This one's especially for you, David: Do you recycle? *(Beat)* Only your milk jugs? Tsk, tsk.

DAVID: *(To GREG)* You don't respect your environment.

GEORGE: When I woke I saw leaves above me, then my Daddy's face, the spit dripping down his chin, right into my eye. He made me crawl back to the truck on my hands and knees, with the barrel of his gun at my ass. But I didn't mind a bit. I was happy. My camel had got away. And I'd been born again by that smile. *(Beat)* Watch this. *(Walks and chews like a camel)*

DAVID: Hey, Greg, were you S D S S? *(Whispers)* Rat-tat-tat-tat. I was.

GREG: *(Whispers)* Secret Desert Storm Supporter? You know, David, that's what I've always appreciated about you liberal types. I mean, recycling not only your clear glass but your green glass as well.

GEORGE: Beautiful, huh? That stride. The stride of a camel. There is nothing else like it.

DAVID: Hey, I care, while you, you've made no choices for the future.

GEORGE: I paste billboards now, and take care of my little bro. But don't think I'm one of those broken-hearted give-ups. I'm watching out for that smile again. You see, unless you are a certain kind of American, you miss the smile, and all those people out there, sneaking their way in here, are out to steal that smile. But over my dead body. That's what I say: over my dead body. *(Itches hump furiously)* It's a sport. *(Beat)* Want another peek at my hump? *(Begins to lift shirt teasingly)* Fuck off. Go get your own. *(Beat)* I'm a camel. *(Chews again)*

(DAVID moves in on GEORGE's space. He pushes GEORGE onto all fours and puts his foot on GEORGE's back. GEORGE doesn't resist.)

DAVID: You, sir, are obviously malfunctioning. Your father shoved a gun barrel up your rectum, so you are also anal retentive.

GEORGE: Anal what?

DAVID: And if a gentleman such as this is anal, it only follows that he'll work the border.

GEORGE: Oink, oink.

DAVID: I never saw a yellow ribbon tied around your tree, George. And I know for a fact that you don't save your newspapers. Did you know that it takes ten years for a seed to become a sapling?

GEORGE: *(Shouts)* This is my story. Mine. Get the fuck out!

GREG: *(To DAVID)* You know, David, this is what gets me. How come you always get to interrupt? Whenever you want?

DAVID: Because you let me?

GEORGE: *(Struggles to his feet)* Fuckin' traitors. Both of you. You're no better than a pair of beaners. Fuckin' beaners, both of you.

DAVID: *(Beat)* George, Greg. This is why I must constantly interrupt you. It's my duty. You see, people like me, we don't call them beaners, wetbacks, or greasers. We who aren't of your, shall we say "constipated class", we call them illegal aliens, immigration offenders, or, for those of us, like myself, still religiously inclined, "poor souls". Try and show a little understanding. I mean, I've used my education to figure it out: We stagnate their economies with our I M F's and can't-pay-them-off-ever loans, so they've got to try and cross and work for Roto-Rooter. Why can't you two be a little more sympathetic? Citizens like myself are trying hard to *(Sings)* reach out and touch someone? This tree, for instance. *(He kneels beside the sapling, sings.)*
I'm the Robin Hood of Saplings
I watch over the small trees
And when I see one broken
It brings me to my knees.
(Beat) At the end of the day, you're still an ignorant man, George, and so are you, Greg, sorry. You don't care about the future, about the air the children of tomorrow will need to breathe. You're selfish, poor, a measly excuse for a working class.

GEORGE: Fuck you. I'm upper working class.

(DAVID *returns to* GEORGE, *smacks* GEORGE *across the face at each word. He does this with measured boredom, and* GEORGE *is passive.*)

DAVID: You *(Smack)* poor, *(Smack)* ignorant *(Smack)* bigot. *(Beat)* Feel any better?

(GEORGE *nods.*)

DAVID: I understand you, George. Your psychological makeup is painfully clear. Nevertheless, you deserve to be punished, as you went ahead and did your show against my better judgment. You're going to have to drag.

GREG: No.

DAVID: George?

GEORGE: I don't want to. It hurts.

DAVID: Learning is painful. *(He takes a small piece of wire from his pocket.)* Open your mouth, George.

GREG: I said no.

DAVID: I heard you. A powerful word, isn't it? "No." "No." "No." Though it depends on who's saying it.*(Beat)* I'm not correcting you, Greg. I'm correcting George.

GREG: I don't want blood on my shirt. That's my shirt he's wearing.

DAVID: Take off the shirt, George.

(GEORGE does so after a moment's reluctance.)

GREG: Put it back on, George.

(GEORGE starts to.)

DAVID: George.

GEORGE: I don't want to drag. It hurts.

GREG: Get back in the car, George.

(No one moves.)

GREG: Not tonight, David. Just this once, do me a favor. I don't think I've asked for one in a while.

DAVID: *(After a silence)* Put the shirt back on, George.

GREG: Thanks. I mean it. Thanks. *(Beat)* Thanks, thanks, thanks. Why am I always thanking you? You pull this every time. Why do you get to decide when and how we do our stuff, where we have to stand?

DAVID: *(Ignores GREG)* No drag, got it, George? But repeat after me: "I am the ignorant one—"

GEORGE: *(Repeats with toleration rather than obedience)* "I am the ignorant one—"

DAVID: "—the humped one—"

GEORGE: "—the humped one—"

DAVID: "—the...the..." *(Snaps his fingers so GREG will give him his line)* Isn't anyone helping out anymore?

GREG: Looks like things are going to hell pretty quick, heh, David?

GEORGE: *(Screams)* I want to finish my story!

DAVID: I give up.

GEORGE: So I hunt Mexicans. It's not a personal thing. Why should I like them? *(Turns to DAVID)* But I like you. You wear nice clothes. You let me mow your lawn.

DAVID: *(Sniffs under his arms)* My armpits are odor free.

GREG: You don't itch your crotch in public.

GEORGE: I mean, how could I hate you when you gave me your old Adidas. and bought my flag for me at K-Mart?

DAVID: So there are no inappropriate feelings?

(GREG shrugs.)

GEORGE: Naw. *(Beat)* Well, how did you like it?

(They ignore him.)

DAVID: *(To GREG)* It's ten o'clock.

GREG: Shut up, George. Let's shift.

GEORGE: Just a fuckin' minute. After you guys went you got some fuckin' feedback. It's my turn now. I get my minute in the sun.

DAVID: But really, Georgie, a camel?

GEORGE: Yeah. A camel.

GREG: *(Laughing now with DAVID)* A camel? I'm tired of this. It's time to move.

GEORGE: Yeah. A camel. Is a camel worth any less than a radish? Than a half-breed with a heart split in two?

DAVID: Have you ever stopped to consider the size of a camel's turd?

GEORGE: O K, O K. But you guys are screwed, because my camel could eat your radish any day. But, you know, I had a rhythm going, and you just moved in, without even asking, and fucked it up.

GREG: You're pathetic, George. You didn't have a rhythm going. You never had a rhythm going.

DAVID: Don't be too hard on him. He's mentally challenged.

GREG: *(Turns on DAVID)* Is he? Well, let's not forget you're only hanging out with us, Mr Educado, due to our good graces. But you know, I think it's time we sent you back to your hot tub.

DAVID: Please. Not that. Let me stay with you fellows. Let me get some dirt on my boots, some oil under my fingernails.

GREG: I've been thinking. All these years I wanted to ask you, but I figured better not because you're my friend. But I want to know. Now. What else? What else from the root family, huh, David? Is it only radishes, or do you get hot over tubers as well? Most of all, did you have the guts to try them out on yourself before you did your sister in?

GEORGE: What's a tuber?

DAVID: A tuber is a situation like this one. Stuck in the ground with no place to grow. Snore, snore. You two Boy Scouts are getting so predictable I'm going to have to go back to playing tennis at the club.

GREG: *(Sniffs* DAVID*)* You know, I've never liked the way you smell.

DAVID: You mean I've practiced all these years for nothing?

GEORGE: What the fuck is up here?

DAVID: Did I ever mention to you two that I finally hired myself a maid?

GEORGE: A beaner?

DAVID: Only the best. Guess what I named her, Greg?

GREG: Maid.

DAVID: Getting warmer.

GEORGE: Cleanie-beanie?

DAVID: Colder.

GREG: I'll tell you what the difference is, David. Like all of them in your club: You wear deodorant, but you can't hide the stink. A real handicap.

DAVID: I gave her a special name. *(Beat)* In honor of Greg, of course.

GEORGE: You see, Greg? He likes you. *(Beat)* Watch this trick: I can eat a rock.

GREG: No. No. I don't want to see you eat a rock. I don't want to see you swallow a beer cap. I don't want to see you put a centipede down your pants. Stop trying to act like a funny guy. You're no more worthless than the rest of us.

GEORGE: I'm not?

GREG: No, you're smart. Sometimes.

GEORGE: I am?

DAVID: This is.... This is.... Words fail me.

GREG: As a matter of fact, you're a winner.

GEORGE: A winner?

GREG: Who spots the most beaners on a weekly basis?

GEORGE: Me?

GREG: Yes. You. Who spots the least?

GEORGE: David.

GREG: And you know why? Because he gets paid not only for the beaners he turns in, but for the ones he lets cross.

GEORGE: Lets cross?

DAVID: Greg.

GREG: As a matter of fact, he gets paid a bonus for the athletic types he lets through. The ones that can do the hard labor.

GEORGE: *(To* DAVID*)* That's not true, is it, David?

DAVID: Hey Greg. About that money you owe me.

GEORGE: You get paid for letting them cross?

DAVID: I think I'll need it by tomorrow.

GEORGE: Why? Why?

GREG: Because David knows he's got to let in just enough beaners to work dead cheap so he can—

DAVID: —maintain my standard of living? It's a very good standard, too. Don't forget it.

GEORGE: I can't believe this.

DAVID: But there's another reason you've left out, Greg. I want to share.

GREG: Share?

DAVID: Certainly. This is the melting pot, isn't it? If we keep everyone out, we'll lose the mix.

GEORGE: You lied to me, David. You never did that to me before.

DAVID: So has Greg. He knew all about it.

GEORGE: Greg?

GREG: If it weren't for David, we wouldn't even have the deal with the Feds to begin with.

GEORGE: Well, fuck you. Fuck you both, I'm going home.

DAVID: *(Takes* GEORGE's *face in his hands)* Hey, I'm still your friend. I've taken good enough care of you so far, haven't I? Who helped you out on your electric bill last month? *(Beat)* You see? I'm still your friend.

*(*GEORGE *pulls away, but less angry now.)*

DAVID: That's right. I am. And I'll tell you what. Just to show you I'm respectable about it, I'm inviting you over so you can finger my new maid's teeth. It will tickle your innards. No charge.

GREG: You really fell for that molar story, didn't you, you *hijo de la gran puta,* son of a bitch.

DAVID: Something tells me that lately you've begun to feel uncomfortable about our relationship.

GREG: No. This isn't a friendship thing. We've always been amigos. Father, Son, and the Holy Ghost, right?

GEORGE: I want to be the ghost. Hey! Look! There's three of them! *(DAVID pays no attention to GEORGE, but GREG is torn between going to help GEORGE and confronting DAVID.)*

DAVID: Then Simon says, "What is it?"

GEORGE: Oh, shit. They're going to charge. Come on, Greg!

GREG: It's how you like it out here.

GEORGE: I like it out here. *(To border)* Go back! Go back! We're not ready for you!

DAVID: Oh, please. Are we going to have another "David thinks he's got gold for shit and only hangs out with us, hoping it will rub off" episodes? Or how about the rerun where you curse me and George for feeling up the chicks we catch just because you haven't got the stomach to join in.

GREG: I never wanted to join in. I just wanted the ten bucks a hit.

GEORGE: Will you two cut the shit and look alive before we lose these guys?

DAVID: Shut up, George. *(To GREG)* Or perhaps you never joined in because of the difficulty you have in getting an erection that will last more than three seconds.

GEORGE: I don't want to talk about Greg's dick!

GREG: *(Refuses to let DAVID "get" him)* If the Feds ever changed their minds, if they ever wanted to burn us...

GEORGE: They fucking crossed.

DAVID: You think they don't know what we're up to? You really are confused.

GEORGE: A hundred feet away from us and we're letting them cross. That's thirty bucks down the drain.

GREG: Well, if they ever did decide to burn us, they'd burn me and George, not you. Not you, because you've got a Lawn-boy rider and a concrete pool.

GEORGE: Let's talk about my show. I want to talk about it!

DAVID: *(To GREG)* My, you are breathing rapidly. You must be ill. Should we call it quits for the night? But we still haven't guessed what I named my maid? *(No response from GREG)* I named her Evalina. *(Beat)* I did it for you. And all I get in return is a—

GREG: *(Interrupts)* You named your maid Evalina? Evalina? Is she one of the chosen ones you let through? I bet she loves her job, doesn't she, cleaning your toilet the same way she brushes her teeth?

DAVID: Teeth. Teeth. It's got into your subconscious, hasn't it, son?

GREG: Tell us how you caught her, David, tell us what you said to her to make her feel safe. Tell us. Which fence line?

DAVID: You're tiresome.

GREG: Did she walk across or did she crawl? What was it like? Hey, David, was it like this?

(GREG *crawls from the border. Though he pretends to be a Mexican woman, it is important that his voice is not affected. He does not try to "sound" like a woman but speaks with his own voice. He may affect a slight accent but then drop it when the action gets more violent.*)

GREG: Hallo! Hallo! Gringo. Do you have a job for me? Gringo. Gringo. Can you help me?

(*As* GREG *speaks,* DAVID *begins to circle* GREG, *joining in the game.*)

DAVID: How can I help you, miss?

GREG: Oh, Mister Gringo. I want to work. I like work.

(DAVID *trips* GREG *and pushes him to his knees.*)

DAVID: So you like to work?

(GEORGE *gets into the game.* DAVID *and* GEORGE *both interrogate* GREG.)

GEORGE: What kind of work?

GREG: Anything. I need money. *Dinero. Dinero.*

DAVID: What for?

GEORGE: What for?

GREG: For pretty clothes?

DAVID: (*Smacks* GREG *in the head*) Stupid answer. Try again. Why do you want money?

GREG: I'm hungry. (*Beat*) I'm starving.

GEORGE: (*Picks up a handful of dirt*) Then open up. I got a McDonald's for you.

(GEORGE *forces dirt in* GREG's *mouth.* GREG *spits it out and attempts to rise.* DAVID *forces him back onto his knees.*)

DAVID: So you want me to give you a job, heh, sweetheart? Why don't you get a nice job in your own hometown?

GEORGE: (*Kicks him*) Yeah. Why do you want to come over here and take mine?

DAVID: You better answer old George, miss, or he'll throw you to the border wolf. (*Beat*) Answer him, you bitch!

GREG: Because... Because...

DAVID: Answer him.

GREG: Because there's no jobs in my hometown. The Yankee pays better over here than the Yankee does over there. *(Beat) Putas. Todos los* Yankees.

DAVID: Did you hear that, George? Cursed at me in Mexican. The bitch.

(DAVID slaps GREG.)

GEORGE: The bitch.

DAVID: But I'm a nice guy. I'll give you a job. You can come home with me. But are you clean?

(GREG holds up his hands to show DAVID that his hands are clean.)

DAVID: Not your hands. I mean what you've got between your legs. Show me.

GREG: No.

GEORGE: Show us.

GREG: No.

GEORGE & DAVID: Show us!

GREG: No!

(DAVID throws GREG on his back and straddles him. GEORGE pins GREG's arms down and puts his hand over GREG's mouth so GREG can't speak.)

DAVID: So you want a job? Well, if you're going to work for me, you can't wear those dirty shirts.

(He rips GREG's shirt open. GREG struggles.)

GEORGE: Nice tits. Look at her tits.

DAVID: What's a girl like you doing in a mess like this? But I will have to give you a tip for your troubles.

(He takes out some dollar bills and stuffs them in GREG's mouth so GREG can't speak.)

GEORGE: Touch her, David. Hurt her. Twist her tit.

(DAVID twists GREG's nipple and GREG screams through the bills.)

DAVID: It's not nice to shout.

(GREG struggles and manages to throw DAVID off of him. Now GREG sits on DAVID. GEORGE has backed off. GREG spits the bills at DAVID's face. There are some moments of silence as DAVID and GREG become aware of their new positions.)

GREG: So you want a job, huh? *(Strikes him hard)* I'm talking to you. You want a job?

GEORGE: Do it again, Greg.

(GREG *strikes* DAVID *again.*)

GREG: Well, if you're going to work for me, you can't wear those fancy shirts. *(Rips* DAVID's *shirt open.* DAVID *is passive, as though stunned.)* Nice, *chica.* Really nice. Here in America—

(GEORGE *pulls on* DAVID's *hair and spits on him.*)

GREG: —we know how to appreciate a nice piece of foreign work. *(Beat)* How does it feel, baby? How does it feel to be on the bottom, with your ass in the dirt? Want to come home with me and scrub my tub? I'll buy you a green apron.

(Some moments of silence)

(As DAVID *speaks the following,* GREG's *power leaves him.)*

DAVID: You know, Greg, I've been meaning to ask you— *(Beat)* —did you ever get that G E D diploma you were working for? You really should, you know. Not that there's anything wrong with not even having a high school diploma, but it is important to be an educated man. That way, you've got more choices. You can move up in the world.

(DAVID *pushes* GREG *off of him.* DAVID *cleans himself off. Neither* GEORGE *nor* GREG *resists him. Then he notices the sapling.)*

DAVID: You fucking clodhoppers. I can't believe it. You stepped on my sapling. Squashed it.

GEORGE: I didn't do it. Greg stepped on it. He did it.

DAVID: Broke its back. You sons of bitches. With your big, dirty, stinking boots. *(Beat)* This night is over. We're calling it quits.

GEORGE: *(Yells)* But I want to have a good time!

GREG: *(Calmly, not shouting)* Aren't you? Aren't you having a good time, George?

DAVID: *(Gazing at sapling)* I don't like to see things die. *(Beat)* Do you remember the taste of your first girl, Greg?

GREG: No. I don't.

DAVID: But you must. How can anyone not remember the taste of their first girl, when you're leaning over to kiss her...

GREG: I don't remember.

DAVID: ...when you're leaning over to kiss her, and her mouth is shining like glass, and her chest is rising and falling when she breathes, rising and falling like the wing of a bird. *(Beat)* But then you hear it again. And it stops you cold. *(He begins to sing.)*

Wrigley Spearmint Radish, Radish, Radish.
Wrigley Spearmint Radish, Radish, Radish.

(GREG *watches him some moments, then begins to shout at* DAVID *until he drowns* DAVID *out. Then* GREG *continues.)*

GREG: Stop. Stop it. Just stop it. *(Beat)* You think that's how it happens? Yeah? You think that's what I remember when I remember my first girl? No, I remember this:

(He slowly, gently runs his finger over DAVID's *lip.* DAVID *does not move or respond.)*

GREG: Evalina. She used to run her finger over my lip like that, and then there was no better place to be than right there where she touched me. *(After a moment of silence, he moves away.)* But that's not how the story gets told, is it, David? Well, I'll tell you right now that I can one-up your radish, you mother fucker. Just watch this. *(Turns to public again, starts out speaking fast)* Hey! Hey! *Dame dos cuchillos.* Throw me a couple of knives. Right here. Think I haven't got it in me? Well, half of me is *mejicano.* The other half of me is WASP. *Come sabes* which side is which? My mother used to tell me: "*Este lado es mejicano.* This side is Mexican, *(Slaps left breast)* the side with the heart." *(Beat)* My father made O K *dinero.* He helped me get a loan on my car. *(Turns to* DAVID*)* Are you listening? *(Back to public/border)* I met my first girl when I was working at the grocers on 17th and Chestnut. She was a chicana.

DAVID: *(Shoves him)* You already told us your *(Beat)* emotional dentistry saga, Greg. No second chances.

GREG: *(Shoves him back)* I figured, like father, like son. And she was legal, nice trailer, two-parent family. *(Beat)* Then she got pregnant. I brought her home to meet my Father.

GEORGE: Hey, I didn't get a second shot. This isn't fair. This isn't fair.

GREG: He called us into his office. I told him: "*Voy a casar con esta chica, Papa.*" It used to piss him off when I spoke Spanish. So, no, I didn't say it like that. I said, "I'd like your permission to marry, sir." He just nodded. Evalina smiled. She'd been so damned loco scared he'd say no. Then he put his hand on Evalina's head and took hold of her long braid. *(Beat)* Then gave her arm a quick twist and she was lying on the floor. She was so surprised, she couldn't make a noise.

(Lifts his foot and balances. GEORGE *and* DAVID *are now listening to him.)*

GREG: No. It's not good enough.

(Suddenly grabs DAVID *by the collar and swings him to the floor)*

GREG: She was so surprised, she couldn't make a noise.

DAVID: *(Protesting)* Hey!

GREG: Shut up.

DAVID: I'm not taking part—

(DAVID breaks off as GREG kicks him violently.)

DAVID: Shut the fuck up! I said: She was so surprised that she didn't make a noise. *(He lifts his foot.)* And then he did this.

(Puts his foot on DAVID's throat. DAVID is passive. GREG speaks as his father.)

GREG: "This isn't the first time I've had to do this. Don't worry about it, son, it's just like getting your finger pricked. Ask your Mother." *(Beat)* And then he brought his boot heel down, hard, on her abdomen. *(Makes a sound of air escaping from his lips)* That was the sound that escaped from Evalina's lips. Can you make that sound, David? *(Jerks DAVID by the hair)* Come on. Try it.

(GREG makes the sound again. DAVID is silent. Then GREG steps over and away from DAVID.)

GREG: Then there was no sound. *Nada. Nada.* I could feel the warm slide of piss running down my leg into my shoe. *Cuando Evalina se despierto*, I drove her home. She was already bleeding it out. *(Beat)* Over breakfast the next morning he asked me...he asked me.... *(He breaks off.)*

DAVID: *(Without malice)* He asked you if you'd decided to postpone the wedding.

GREG: Yeah. *(Beat)* Well, it was a year later. I hadn't been home in a while. I came by to visit my mother. Father was out on patrol. We were just talkin' shop while she was doing the wash. I asked her why she never had any more kids after me. She just shrugged. I came right out and told her about me and Evalina, about almost having to marry, about Father helping us out. I watched her pour a whole bottle of detergent in the wash. Then she said, like she might be saying "That's the third load today", "I thought mine were the only ones". Then she hit me.

(He moves to DAVID, takes DAVID's hand, and uses it to smack himself in the face. Then DAVID tunes in on the role and now DAVID plays GREG's Mother, but with no affectations in his voice.)

DAVID: And you did nothing? *(Smacks GREG again)* And you did nothing? *(Smacks GREG again, harder)* And you did nothing?

GREG: The kid would have been three fourths beaner, Ma. Not a hundred percent, like you, but three fourths. Three fourths. An almost. A not quite. A partly. A fuckin' percentage. And he'd never be able to grow up and be like his father, Ma. Like I can never grow up and be like you, no matter how hard I try. *(He moves to GEORGE.)* She spit at me.

(GREG is expecting GEORGE to spit at him. When he doesn't, GREG pushes him.)

GREG: *(Louder)* She spit at me. Hey! *(Pushes him)* Hey!

(GEORGE spits him in the face. GREG turns his story back to the public.)

GREG: That's right. *(quietly)* When my father walked through the door that night, "bang", my mother shot him in the throat, bull's-eye through the adam's. *(Sings)*
Oh, Evalina, no llores mas por mi
Porque vamanos to the border
Con cervezas cross my knee
So I'm here. The border. It keeps me in line. I mean, what if I just gave up this huntin'? I might start going weird.

GEORGE: Quit it, Greg.

GREG: I mean, I might start feeling sorry for Evalina again, go track her down. Find out where she went to.

DAVID: Enough of this old boy.

GREG: I might even take that gun of his I've got hidden under a floorboard in my room.

GEORGE: *(Becoming more agitated)* Stop it!

GREG: I might go out hunting. But maybe not for beaners this time.

GEORGE: I can't listen to you anymore!

GREG: And what if I got even weirder and went after some of you too. I don't know. I mean, you saw him lift his foot over her belly, didn't you? *(Laughs, turns to DAVID and GEORGE and says calmly)* And you did nothing? *(Turns back to public/border)* And you did nothing? *(Beat)* And you did nothing?

GEORGE: Shut the fuck up!

GREG: I mean, he was the law, your law, and she was just the cheap labor.

(GEORGE punches GREG in the face. GREG falls down.)

DAVID: Get the fuck back in the car or this will be the last time we take you shopping.

(GREG gets up as though obeying DAVID and goes to the car, but then he snatches the gun. GREG raises the gun and aims at them.)

GEORGE: No, Greg. Put that down.

DAVID: Stay calm, big boy. Take a deep breath.

GREG: *(Speaks calmly and with complete assurance)* Shut up. You're both dead. *(Beat)* Hey, I look good, don't I?

DAVID: Brilliant.

GREG: I've never been more brilliant in all my life. *(Beat)* You're finished. Both of you.

DAVID: Listen, Greggie.

GREG: No. I'm not going to listen. You're going to listen.

GEORGE: Jesus, Greg.

DAVID: You're not playing the game.

GREG: But I am. *(Beat)* Trust me. *(Beat)* Hey, let's play one more time? Which one should we play, David? Once upon a time in the land of radishes?

DAVID: Listen to me a minute. If you'd just—

GREG: *(Interrupts)* No. Not that one. We're tired of that one. So tell me, David, how do you spell relief? *(Beat)* My story is about halves. *(Lifts shirt)* Will you look at this? Split down the middle. But which side is which? I mean, when the moment hit you, when the crisis struck, which did you choose, Hostess or Sara Lee? J V C or Sony? I mean, isn't that the simple beauty of it: Who can afford to hire a maid and who can't afford not to be one?

(GEORGE moves slightly, as though he is thinking to run for it.)

GEORGE: Let me go, Greg. I got to get home.

GREG: Hey, don't you want to play a game? This is your game, David. I say the words and you try and put your mind to work somewhere else so the words won't get to you. Now, think hard about the first time you put your tongue in someone else's mouth, or map it out in your head how you're gonna change things in your neighborhood. Or how about this one: picture how your sister looked when you left her lying there in the park, saying: *(Softly)* No. *(Beat)* David. No. David. No. *(Slaps* DAVID *in the face, though not hard.* DAVID *is passive.)* David. No. *(Beat)* Now, I dare you not to switch out, not to turn off. O K? "I pledge allegiance, to the flag, of the United...." Hold it. Let's start over. Make it harder this time. *(Pokes him with the gun)* Hey. Pay attention. Isn't this what you taught me?

(He puts the gun in DAVID'*s hand and places the gun at his own forehead. They are both holding it now.)*

GREG: Come on, David. Show us your stuff. *(He kneels.)* "I pledge allegiance, to the flag of the United States of—

(Knocks DAVID *so* DAVID *says the rest of the pledge with him.)*

GREG & DAVID: —America. And to the Republic for which it stands, one nation, under God, indivisible, with *(Beat)* liberty and justice for all."

(Stands and takes the gun back from DAVID*)*

GREG: David. No. *(Beat)* The show's over. *(Beat)* O-V-E-R! *(Beat)* George, get out of here.

(GEORGE doesn't move. GREG speaks gently.)

GREG: Hey, now and then, you were funny. I mean it. *(Beat)* So go home, Camel-boy. *(To DAVID)* But I can't let you off that easy, David. Yeah, I like you. But I'm your nightmare now, your very own one-hundred-percent All American, pure beef Wetback, and I'm gonna stay right here, light up this border, *(Beat)* but how about from the other side this time. *(Beat)* Y de ahora en adelante ya no voy a hablar mas el ingles. Yo necesito mis proprias palabras para..para...luchar. Si, ya se que has escuchado todo eso antes, pero esto vez...Watch out!

(Pushes DAVID to kneel. DAVID does not resist. GREG pulls DAVID's head back by the hair and kisses him violently on the forehead.)

GREG: Listen. Something just had to give. It's nothing personal. *(Raises gun to DAVID's temple. GREG speaks calmly and slowly.)* We were always friends.

(There are some moments of silence as we wait for the shot. Nothing happens.)

GREG: *Escucha*, David. With all that *inteligente* you bought— *(Holds the gun up in front of DAVID's face)* —can you read this? Right here? Can you read it? It doesn't say Taiwan or Japan this time. On the barrel, you can read it if you squint. You see what it says? *(He steps back from the two of them.)* It says: Made in the U S A. *(Beat)* Here. *(Holds out gun to DAVID and GEORGE)* You can have it back.

(Neither GEORGE nor DAVID moves. GREG drops the gun at their feet. He begins to exit. Lights black out just as he leaves the stage.)

END OF PLAY